AF267342

You are. That is.

Creative

Finding your way to your greater creative self

noula diamantopoulos

National Library Catalogue
Creator   : Diamantopoulos, Noula, author.
Title   : You are. That is. Creative
                 finding your way to your greater creative self /
                 Noula Diamantopoulos.
ISBN   : 9780994510709 (paperback)
ISBN   : 9780994510716 (ebook)
Subjects   : Creative ability–Popular works.
                 Creative thinking–Popular works.
                 Creation (Literary, artistic, etc.)–Popular works.
Dewey Number : 153.35

Book Details
Designer   : Natalie Behjan
Publishing Consultants/
Interior Design : Pickawoowoo Publishing Group

Publisher
Studio Noula
Sydney Australia

For enquiries, write to: rights and permissions via publisher.
www.nouladiamantopoulos.com

This book is dedicated to my parents

Emily Rose Diamantopoulos

Michael Diamantopoulos

When you both left, I became aware of your teachings.
They are beautiful.

Prologue

This book has one simple message. You are creative.

Being creative… means that you are inquisitive and curious about life and about who you are, that you value the power of your imagination to navigate your life's choices and challenges, that you see the world through an expansive lens of possibility and that you voice the language of poetry to uplift our spirits and enrich our lives.

Being creative… means that you remember to allow the light into your heart by inviting playfulness and allowing timidity to lapse into oblivion as you laugh out loud – usually at yourself.

Being creative… means that you give yourself permission to be embarrassed in your attempts to create while you patiently await those moments when you will amaze yourself and then let a smile greet your face and celebrate with your newfound strut.

Being creative… doesn't go away just because things get hard or you're not having fun, or that you feel like hiding under the covers, or to take a nap to be alone and to sometimes do nothing.

Being creative… who would you be if you weren't?

Contents

Unfolding Your Personal Creative Process

The Quest

The Creative Journey

That Is. Creative

You Are. Creative

The Poem

Ithaka

As you set out for Ithaka

hope the road is long,

full of adventures, full of knowledge.

The Laestrygonians and the Cyclops,

angry Poseidon – do not fear them,

you will never find these things on your way,

if your thoughts remain lofty, if fine

emotion touches your spirit and your body.

The Laestrygonians and the Cyclops,

the fierce Poseidon – you will never encounter,

unless you carry them inside your soul,

unless your soul sets them up in front of you.

Hope for the road to be long.

May there be many summer mornings

when with such pleasure, such joy

you come into harbours seen for the very first time;

may you stop at Phoenician markets

and purchase fine goods,

mother of pearl and coral, amber and ebony,

and all kinds of sensual perfumes,

as many sensual perfumes as possible;

may you visit many Egyptian cities,

to learn and learn from the scholars.

Always keep Ithaka in your mind.

Arriving there is what you are destined for.

But do not hurry the journey at all.

Better it lasts many years;

and you arrive an old man on the island,

wealthy with all that you have gained on the way,

not expecting Ithaka to give you riches.

Ithaka gave you the beautiful voyage.

Without her you would have never set out.

She has nothing more to give you now.

And if you find her poor, Ithaka hasn't deceived you.

Wise as you will have become, with such experience,

you will have understood by then what Ithakas mean.

C.P Cavafy, 1911

Translated by Matina Spetsiotis

ΙΘΑΚΗ

Σα βγεις στον πηγαιμό για την Ιθάκη,
να εύχεσαι νά'ναι μακρύς ο δρόμος,
γεμάτος περιπέτειες, γεμάτος γνώσεις.
Τους Λαιστρυγόνας και τους Κύκλωπας,
τον θυμωμένο Ποσειδώνα μη φοβάσαι,
τέτοια στον δρόμο σου ποτέ σου δεν θα βρεις,
αν μέν' η σκέψις σου υψηλή, αν εκλεκτή
συγκίνησις το πνεύμα και το σώμα σου αγγίζει.
Τους Λαιστρυγόνας και τους Κύκλωπας,
τον άγριο Ποσειδώνα δεν θα συναντήσεις,
αν δεν τους κουβανείς μες στην ψυχή σου,
αν η ψυχή σου δεν τους στήνει εμπρός σου,

Να εύχεσαι νά'ναι μακρύς ο δρόμος.
Πολλά τα καλοκαιρινά πρωιά να είναι
που με τι ευχαρίστησι, με τι χαρά
θα μπαίνεις σε λιμένας πρωτοειδωμένους·
να σταματήσεις σ' εμπορεία Φοινικικά,
και τες καλές πραγμάτειες ν' αποκτήσεις,
σεντέφια και κοράλλια, κεχριμπάρια κ' έβενους,
και ηδονικά μυρωδικά κάθε λογής,
όσο μπορείς πιο άφθονα ηδονικά μυρωδικά·
σε πόλεις Αιγυπτιακές πολλές να πας
να μάθεις και να μάθεις απ' τους σπουδασμένους.

4

Πάντα στον νου σου νά 'χεις την Ιθάκη.
Το φτάσιμον εκεί είν' ο προορισμός σου.
Αλλά μη βιάζεις το ταξείδι διόλου.
Καλλίτερα χρόνια πολλά να διαρκέσει·

και γέρος πια ν' αράξεις στο νησί,
πλούσιος με όσα κέρδισες στον δρόμο,
μη προσδοκώντας πλούτη να σε δώσει η Ιθάκη.

Η Ιθάκη σ' έδωσε τ' ωραίο ταξείδι.
Χωρίς αυτήν δεν θα 'βγαινες στον δρόμο.
Άλλα δεν έχει να σε δώσει πια.

Κι αν πτωχική την βρεις, η Ιθάκη δεν σε γέλασε.
Έτσι σοφός που έγινες, με τόση πείρα,
ήδη θα το κατάλαβες η Ιθάκες τι σημαίνουν.

Κ. Π. Καβάφης, 1911

Introduction

I have no doubt in my mind or heart that we are all creative beings. We cannot not be. This is my truth. I have witnessed the most hardened disbelievers, people who have no faith in their own creativity transform and, as a result of the transformation, they experience an awakened life filled with the potential to always discover more. Creativity is a never-ending story.

Ashley didn't believe she was creative when she signed up to my introductory course, The Creative Shaman. She is a career woman who joined the class to break away from all her left-brain thinking. Her career was exhausting her mentally and emotionally and she felt she had nothing left to give. Her weekends were spent relaxing, where she could, from the long work hours, but then there was the shopping and the housekeeping. Any time left over was precious and she wanted to share that time with her partner, her family and her friends, but even spending time with loved ones had now become a chore. Her solution was to come to my art class. It was a small commitment: meeting for three hours one evening a week for six weeks. This was time out for her. A time where she could focus on herself and no-one else.

During the first night of class, we began to discuss the meaning of the word 'creative'. She felt uneasy with the topic and was unable to articulate what she thought or believed, except that she believed without a doubt, that she could not draw and was not creative.

This is not unusual. Many people associate the word creative exclusively with the visual arts. An expansive view of the word creative would show that everything we do and say is an act of creativity. Our actions and words create relationships and not just things that hang on walls.

There are many creative tools and processes that I use to access someone's quietly waiting creativity. Working with the non-dominant hand, turning drawings and initial paint marks sideways and starting again, meditations and developing an intuitive approach are some of my favourite 'ways' to overcome blocks, stagnation and to allow something new to come through. I asked Ashley to draw an apple from memory with her non-dominant hand. She laughed, saying that she couldn't control that hand so how could she expect to draw something without being able to control it. I agreed with her and suggested that it was just a bit of fun and she should feel relaxed because there was no pressure or even hope that her apple would look any good. She began to draw and then stopped. She was looking for her eraser. As soon as she found it I asked her to give it to me and to please continue drawing without it. She continued and, a few moments later when she had finished, she said "It looks more like a tomato."

"That's great", I said.

She didn't agree. "But now you know how to draw a tomato. Do you like your tomato?"

"Yes, but it's meant to be an apple?"

"Does it matter?"

"Well, yes."

"Why?"

"Because that's not what you wanted me to draw."

"I understand and we can get back to drawing an apple, but right now you know how to draw a tomato and you like what you drew, right?"

"Yes, I guess."

"And you did it from memory, not from looking at one, without an eraser and using your non-dominant hand."

"Oh yeah, I did!"

"Shall we try an apple now?"

We are creative. We have a particular way of creating. We each have our own visual language when it comes to drawing and painting and all the visual arts. We all have our own ways of speaking and writing when it comes to prose and poetry. We each have our own individual taste buds when it comes to cooking. We each have a special way of seeing the world and expressing ourselves in the modality we choose and this individual way we each have, will always be an act of creativity.

When I start the creative journey with a beginner, the very first lessons are about not needing to know about colour theory, not needing to know about technique, not needing to know how to hold a brush or a pencil. First I want people to see that they can already create. I want to show people what's within them. Pick up the pencil and draw, pick up the brush and just choose a colour intuitively, use your smart phone and take some photos – shoot from the hip, literally, to capture a different viewpoint and then write a story about it. These are the ways that I engage with you to help you to release what is locked up within. And there it is - **You Are** (yes, you are) and **That Is** (what you create always will be) **Creative**.

About The Poem Ithaka

I have read the poem *Ithaka* by Cavafy to almost every class that I have run since I began to teach art classes almost two decades ago. I ask my students to close their eyes, to sit back in their chairs and to focus on their breath for a moment. Then I read *Ithaka* out loud to them, pausing for emphasis in different places. When they reopen their eyes, the students look refreshed and relaxed, as if they had been on a holiday. They have taken the time to enjoy an imaginary voyage. This is Cavafy's wisdom. To pause. To elongate the journey and know that this is life's gift to us.

I call this the Ithaka Effect. It is the simple notion that your adventure begins the moment you focus on where you want to go – you don't have to wait to get to your destination before you allow yourself to feel joy. Just like my students who arrive at an art class. Their journey began when the idea of joining an art class crossed their mind. Then the excitement builds to find the class that feels right to them. And it continues as they buy the materials in preparation for their first lesson. These students are filled with anticipation and joy and they haven't even started the class yet. Ithaka is about enjoying the journey that the decision to enroll in an art class has taken you on. And once you have decided on what your destination is, what your Ithaka is, your conversations change. They incorporate the new path that you are now on. Your anticipation and preparation for this new journey spills into all areas of your life. As you attend your art classes and take the steps towards making and creating, the journey takes you sideways, up ways, start-again-ways and you end up in unexpected places that you might never have encountered had you not taken action on the initial spark, the pulse of an idea of joining an art class.

Mary is in her mid-60s and was given my beginners' art course by her daughters. She was shy entering the classroom. Mary felt out of sorts and yet there was a part of her that was willing to give the course a go. Each time an exercise was completed and we went around the room to share the students' creative efforts, Mary would start with an apology "I'm sorry, I don't think I understood the exercise." "I'm sorry, I feel that I failed to get the lines right." "I'm sorry, it's not a very good painting, the colours are all wrong."

Each and every time I would tell her gently that there was no need to apologise. After several weeks of self-condemnation I decided to go on a crusade for her creativity. I knew that if Mary continued to put down her creative efforts then pretty soon her creative potential would shy away to oblivion.

The next time Mary apologised for her work I asked "Mary, are you sorry you are here? Are you sorry that you are attending this course?" "No no, not at all" she said, "I am enjoying this more than anything I have done in a long time. I have spent so much time caring for others. This is my time now." "Okay," I said, "can I know why you keep apologising for your work? Are you ashamed of your abilities?" Mary stared into my eyes. "I'm not sure why I do that. I feel I should be better than I am. I feel that if I am following your instructions correctly I should be producing something I can be proud of." "Oh, I see," was my response. "So did you come to art classes to learn to draw and paint or did you come to art classes to show others that you can create beautiful work in the first instance?" "But shouldn't my work look beautiful if I follow your instructions correctly." "Oh sure," I said. "Like when I asked you to draw a self-portrait with your non-dominant hand while juggling a small shaving mirror in your other hand. Do you remember? That's when I asked that you tape the drawing paper down on your board and you were not allowed to take the pencil off the paper. Why would I ask a beginner to do that? It was for you to experience the ability to look at your own face without judgement and to capture the grace of an unbroken line, a line that has recorded your hands every movement every step which, by the way, you did beautifully. Is it possible that you are unclear on the role of art exercises? Art exercises are designed to train your eye and your thoughts to see and think differently? The end result is intended to be a learning not a masterpiece." Mary began to smile. She also asked me to repeat what I had said so she could write it down to take home with her to reread whenever she felt focused on the end result instead of the journey.

And here we return to the poem by Cavafy, *Ithaka*, that acts as a reminder of the well-turned phrase "It's the journey that matters not the destination." What does that mean anyway?

Ithaka is a Greek Island. You read about Ithaka and a desire stirs to go there. Excitement mounts. Preparations are made. Conversations are all about the journey. Plans get underway and you buy a ticket to go to Ithaka.

You are now on board a ship travelling the wide-open seas and you stop at ports along the way and learn new things and see art and processes that you have never seen before. New people board at each port and others disembark. There is loss and also the birth of new friendships. You continue along the way and storms and high waters hit the boat. You experience what it is like to be in the hands of the forces of nature. No one can steer the boat to safety. And then there are long stretches of quiet and calm and sunshine and no land in sight. You begin to wonder if you made the right decision to take this trip. Self-doubt sets in and fear runs through your veins. You come face to face with your inner demons and then you reach another port. Your soul is renewed and your heart sings. Many years have passed. You have seen so much. You have experienced so much. And you arrive in Ithaka. That was the gift: To take the voyage in the first place.

Who Is This Book For?

When I first began to write this book, I was writing for myself. For me as a teacher who facilitates the emergence of someone else's creativity. For me as a psychotherapist who facilitates the emergence of the dormant better version of oneself. And for me personally, to understand what it is that I do outside these labels. Well, that's how it started. And when I did begin this book it was called The Ithaka Effect. After the first polished draft of the book was completed, my dear friend Kaye Fallick said "But I want it to be about me. How do I become more creative? I want some practical tips about the Ithaka Effect. I want to know how to get there. Give me some exercises please." So here it is. **You Are. That Is. Creative** is a book about how to keep your imagination alive and active so that you can become the greater creative being that you inherently are.

The way I came to write this book has proved to be perfect for me. I could not have written a book for you if I had not written it first for me. In a way, the writing of this book has proven to be my own journey to Ithaka.

And, pragmatically, this book is for all who are new to the arts, all those wanting to try out as an artist or who are simply trying to approach art without fighting through the barrage of fear that almost automatically comes when you enter the dominion of the arts.

This book is also for counsellors and psychotherapists who want to include creative processes in their practice. And finally it is for those who wish to live a greater creative life whether this involves the visual arts or not.

So this book is for you. You who have attempted to overcome your concerns about making art, about creating, about being creative and about finding your greater creative self in this process. This is a book for you.

Yearning To Make Art

I have a workshop called The Creative Shaman, which grew out of a previous workshop called Art For Strictly Beginners. This is one of my signature courses and attracts people who are truly beginners to feel comfortable to try their hand at art skills, to learn how to paint and draw. Yet I find that people mostly come to these courses wanting to find out whether they are creative or not. I know this because on the first night of the course I ask participants why they have enrolled and what they want to get out of the course. Over a period of 18 years there has been little change in what people would say. This perplexed me. Why were they relying on my course, or any other art course for that matter, to determine whether or not they were creative, whether they had a natural talent or an innate ability to draw? Why do we expect creativity to be genetic like the colour of our hair rather than a learnable skill like reading or writing? Why weren't they coming just to learn art?

How to begin to make art? Where to start the journey? Do I go to art school? Which art school and what will I learn? This was me in the beginning:

I had left an 18-year career as an international tax manager on the strength of a calling for the arts. I had never painted before, nor had I ever had a desire to do so. Prior to this stirring towards the arts, I didn't even like attending art exhibitions. I simply wasn't interested at looking at paintings hanging on a wall. And yet... something had awakened in me and what surfaced was not the discovery of a hidden talent. On the contrary, what I uncovered was a deeply buried desire to express myself. I write these words now but admit that at the time I didn't know what this 'desire to express myself' actually meant. How could I have a sense of wanting something but no sense of what that something actually was?

That was mostly because I didn't really know much about

myself, about who I was. Of course I knew the obvious things about myself like the personal qualities and skills I brought to my profession as an accountant and an international tax advisor. I had certainty because I was evaluated every year by my superiors and peers and my career performance was measured against my KPIs. I knew about my good standing as a family member for I felt included and loved by my whole family (well most of the time). I knew about my strong competitive streak which came through playing volleyball, basketball, squash and every other sport I competed in. All of this self-knowledge came from outside of me. I knew myself through competing against others, through assigned goals that were externally set and through the good opinion of others! Always the good opinion of others, always measured against external review.

I wanted to paint. I didn't know why and I didn't know what, however I felt pulled toward the raw linen canvas and the wooden panel and the feel of paint moving across their surfaces, unfolding a mythical story. I was and still am fascinated by this process. Can I call it that? Is there a process?

I explored what the art schools had to offer. Surely I didn't need to do another degree? I was a year away from completing my second degree, this time in law, and I wasn't convinced that another degree would teach me how to become an artist.

Technical colleges were the way. They were hands-on and practical. Trial and error became my process. That's what I learnt from all the classes I took and all the teachers I had over the next two years – and the worst thing I learnt was the attitude that typified the arts world. I had left one competitive environment for another. This time, this super ego was underpinned by ideas of what is good art, what is bad art, what is great art, and God forbid what is craft.

I studied and learned techniques from practising artists too. Some of these were short weekend workshops and others were year-long programs. I was also teaching myself through books and experimentation. This was when I began to teach art too. As I was learning I was also teaching. I leased a studio space in 1998 and then in 2000 I moved into my current studio where I teach art and personal growth workshops. By 2003, I had discovered that my personal journey was to be taken within. I studied meditation and spiritual philosophies. I began to coach people and then enrolled in a holistic psychotherapy course and graduated as a psychotherapist and that's when my art practice turned inside out as I began a process of un-processing, of dissolving all the rules of art and art-making that I had consciously and unconsciously adopted. I hoisted a new flag of independence, white like a blank canvas, and began again.

I un-processed everything I knew about painting, about mixing colour, about brushes and mediums and styles and techniques. It sounds absurd. How do you pretend to not know something you already know? It's like saying to someone, "Don't think of a pink elephant in a tutu." Of course that's the only thing you can see! But wait! I've skipped a whole lifetime of stories about what happened in between the start of my emerging art career and where I am now.

In my early years of painting there emerged a naiveté that I loved. Wonderfully emotive paintings of faces, strong painted line work and saturated colours. And that's where I felt I failed. It was in the addition of colour. Somehow, I would lose the strength in the line because I substituted a need for colour to be applied the way I had learnt about it and the theory of complements. This knowledge, which was taught in art schools and was designed to impart and to build confidence in the emerging artist, had the opposite effect on me. I didn't realise it at the time. I simply believed that I lacked talent when it came to applying colour. I hadn't noticed that the art knowledge I had picked up was stifling me. I am not suggesting that this happens to all students of the arts, but it did happen to me. I wasn't seeing colour for myself anymore. I was seeing colours for the way they should go together, seeking out and replicating recipes and losing touch with my inner connection with the work being produced. I didn't know how to begin a relationship with my materials. I was in awe of the thousands of great paintings already created by well-known artists. I was even in awe of the other students' work – they weren't famous but somehow their paintings surpassed mine.

I was held back by what I saw as art, past and present. I didn't understand the processes, nor what pushed those artists to make art. In truth, I didn't understand the visual arts beyond the notion of some kind of self-expression, which meant very little to me (remember, I didn't have a sense of inner self back then). I was lost in the dangerous and hidden conviction that only people with talent can draw, paint, sculpt, write.

That last statement is simply not true. I know that now. I have studied the stories of many of the greats and know of their personal struggles and the repetitive process required to master painting or writing – or golf strokes for that matter.

The difference with the achievements of athletes is that we can see that they have worked out because their physique is an indication of their commitment and time spent training. Yet with the visual artist and writer we do not see their struggles, the thousands of words that have fallen off the pages, which have been subject to correction again and again. Or the number of sketches an artist makes to create one final artwork. Nor the daily attempts to balance colour on canvases or the number of underpaintings that lie below the painting that is visible, let alone the canvases that have ended up wasted and thrown out with the trash.

Art is a practice and that's what it looks like when you are practising. When I used to learn Greek dancing I would start a new dance routine and my feet would move leftwards instead of right and as they tried to autocorrect, my knees would knock together almost bringing my body to the floor. If you know anything about Greek dancing you will know that the feet move sideways, backwards, forwards and turn and twist and half-twist. Once you have the routine down pat then of course it's elegant to witness the movements as well as to dance them, yet when I was learning a new routine it was as if my feet were dyslexic. And then something mysterious happened: I would come to practice as usual and my legs knew exactly what to do. No more fumbling or trying to pretend that I wasn't going left when I was meant to be going right. If you are musical then you must have your own stories of when you first began to learn an instrument. At some point something happens between the brain and the body movement – that chord you were trying to get your fingers to remember over the keyboard or the guitar strings, all that practice, all those mistakes, became a fluid movement and voilá!

Practising Starts

My yearning to make art eventually became a yearning to make my own art. I no longer wished to represent my outer world. I wanted to bring out what I sensed internally, to see what was stirring within me. That pull towards my inner world was far stronger than any need to prove to someone else that I had any talent. What a strange thing to say! Yet this is the best way I can describe what finding (though I was still searching at this point) your voice feels like. It brings about a silent confidence that you are meant to be doing what you are doing, that your distinctive signature in brush marks, your singular way of seeing colours interplay and intermingle, your individual approach in the way you speak and write, must be allowed to blossom. This is a must. If you do not pursue the pulse of this must, you will not get to explore the sea beyond the shores of a safe harbour of what is popular and what is acceptable.

Practise moving away from the shoreline. Practise starting. Do it again and again, each time moving further and further towards the place beckoning to you – the pulse of the 'must'.

Continue, even if you feel you are going in the wrong direction. You cannot know until you move out of sight of the shoreline. Withdraw from what you already know and allow yourself the opportunity to uncover what is already there waiting for you – your voice.

My artwork starts as a response to the medium that I feel called to. I work in a variety of mediums so I am used to how it feels to be called by my art material. Sometimes I imagine the texture of the canvas, I sense the brush moving a luscious luminous hue over the ridges created by the woven cotton, the warp and weft. At other times I imagine my hands moving through the wet clay, my left hand pulls the clay backwards and the right holds the remaining clay in place and something begins to grow. At other times I hear a word, or read a line from a book I am studying, a quote I have stumbled across or even something

I said in class when I was teaching, a statement or thought that is as new to me as it may be to my students; a thought that I am so curious about that I am compelled to follow.

If it is clay that calls me, then it is about pushing the form, experimenting with it. I say experimenting yet it feels more like experiencing the clay. Both words are true because I don't know what will end up being produced (experiment) but I do know that I am responding to the feeling of the clay moving between my two hands (experience).

Each medium calls out to something within me and I often work in more than one medium at a time.

But right now it is about painting. I feel pulled toward the raw linen canvas and the wooden panels. I can see them leaning against one of my studio doors as I write these pages on my computer. They are waiting for me to come, to pick them up, to place them on the easel. They are asking me to explore and move into their whiteness.

What will move into this whiteness, I'm not sure yet… until suddenly I feel a flow of colours – colours like turquoise and pink and light yellow and lime.

These colours have a mythical story to unfold. That's what I am pursuing. That's what gets me started and then keeps me going. Even if I were to pick a subject like portraits, the depictions of those faces on the canvas, the lines that make them up and the shapes that form them, are really only there to capture and create a space for colour. I could as easily paint colour within the shape of bottles like Giorgio Morandi.

Giorgio Morandi, an artist who for the greater part of his career painted bottles – bottles and jugs and maybe the occasional bowl. Morandi's canvases were small, often only around 30 x 40cm, the paint hardly covering the entire surface. What did he want from these bottles? That question took me on an inner voyage: what was Morandi's intention? I sat in meditation and imagined Morandi in his home where he painted in Bologna in Italy. I imagined a tall, thin man smoking a roll-your-own cigarette held with three fingers, puffing the smoke out and contemplating his small canvas. How odd, the size of the canvas compared to his stature. As I communed with Morandi I imagined him moving his brush across the canvas and the bottles simply became vessels. The vessels held space for him. They were no longer bottles. I began to reflect on the repetitiveness of painting the same shape over and over. At some point this continual, seemingly monotonous, repetition of bottles dissolved the notion of bottle entirely and they became vessels of light. Morandi was exploring light. Ultimately he used bottles in his still life compositions as a way to capture spaces of light and dark in colour.

If we are called on to express ourselves, then the key element in that statement is 'ourselves'. To express something of self. Of course learn from others, but the way to learn from them is to understand their motivation, their quest. For what they have created is in response to their quest.

My eyes open and I begin painting afresh. I select my palette and am ready to begin.

How Is This Book Set Out?

There are three parts to this book, which can be read in any sequence. The three parts are:

Unfolding Your Personal Creative Process, The Quest and **The Creative Journey**. I have named each section to reflect the various stages and aspects of a personal journey, as in the poem *Ithaka*.

The first part of the book is called **Unfolding Your Personal Creative Process.** This is a five-part process that generates an interior map which reveals your own innately creative way of navigating this planet. It is your modus operandi. We all have a means of thinking and feeling our way through what we want to be or do in life. This personal way, this personal navigational style is, curiously, the same whether we are problem-solving or starting a new painting. Your interior map will show you how you direct your life right now and whether you steer towards what you want or away from what you don't want. You will get to know yourself better and to appreciate yourself, your strengths, qualities and traits. You will be able to see what you value in life and what's important to you. Too often we tend to remember what we are not good at, maybe because we spend more time trying to hide that rather than throwing light onto our strengths. Time to shift gear!

The second part of the book is called **The Quest** and it is a technique in asking questions. I created Quest as a performance artwork, a part of my art practise and have performed it in public spaces and corporate settings. If you are interested in seeing me perform Quest, I have it recorded on video, which you can view on www.noulaquesting.blogspot.com.au

I believe we do not spend enough time articulating a question and when we don't we end up with a rapscallion question that takes us on a wild goose chase. While this may be an amusing adventure, it will not help you shed light on what you are truly seeking to Quest on. What's more, it may actually have a limiting effect on your search because you are looking for an answer to the wrong question.

All journeys begin when our curiosity is nudged. Welcome or unwelcome, the nudge hangs around waiting for us to pay attention. If we don't listen to the nudge it becomes a push, and later a shove, until it is heard. When we do finally listen to that inner niggling, our imagination is activated and questions begin to form. It is at this point that we want to discern which question is the one that will act as a motivator for passionate action. The right question acts like rocket fuel, propelling us towards what we deeply desire.

Here is how Quest works: it is a series of questions exchanged between two people. No answers are given. The primary questor starts with a question written on a piece of paper which is then given to the companion questor. The companion questor responds with another question. At the outset you can set a time limit, say 15 minutes or a question limit, say five questions each. This interchange of written questions is completed in silence. The silence intensifies the experience and encourages the questors to a) investigate the meaning of each other's questions, b) think through a response in question format and c) articulate it.

At a recent art performance of Quest I had made cards to hand out to people attending a private exhibition opening. Many art collectors were drinking champagne and eating canapés. I was dressed all in white and handed out printed cards that said 'Will You QUEST-ion me?' On the back of the card were printed the words you, me, you, me. I wasn't certain that my performance would catch the interest of any of the collectors, but I created a buzz. At first people thought this was a playful, light-hearted game. And it can be that. But not when I am Questing you! One tall, vivacious young woman came towards me and wanted to participate. I gave her the card and she wrote down her first question which was "Are you happy?" Here is how the rest of the questions went. My responses are in italic.

Would you believe me if I told you?

Shouldn't I believe you?

Who is the best person to answer that question?

Is it you?

When will you learn to trust yourself?

This particular performance was designed to not take up too much time, so we only had three questions each. In the above example, in three short questions each, we came to a very curious place. When she read the last question she paused and looked at me and said "This technique works." She walked away slowly and then stopped, looked back at me and smiled.

Here is another example:

Can I learn to draw?

Do you want to learn to draw?

How can I know that I am talented?

Do you need talent to draw?

How can I know that I am creative?

Who has the authority to award a person the title talented?

What do you do when you are scared of being judged?

Why do you care about other people's opinions?

Doesn't everybody care about other people's opinions?

What do you think about yourself?

In the above Quest you can see in 10 short shared questions that self-doubt was lurking behind the desire to learn to draw. Self-awareness helps a person understand that their ability to learn to draw may be affected by negative beliefs and doubts about their talent. Knowing this or becoming aware of this helps to adjust the compass towards where they really need to steer. Perhaps instead of enrolling in an art course described as 'beginners welcomed' they should take one called for beginners only.

The final part of the book is called **The Creative Journey**. This is a series of log notes or musings on the topics, issues and matters that are concurrently, like the proverbial baggage, travelling with you. I have divided the musings into two sections – *That Is. Creative* is about the creative process and *You Are. Creative* is about you and what might be stopping you from believing you are creative. The topics covered, such as self-doubt, the inner critic and judgment, the way we define the nature of creativity and talent, have a universal relevance. My approaches are art-based and use tools from my psychotherapy practice such as mindfulness and meditation. There are no answers in these log notes. They are reflections from my almost 20 years of educating in the arts and from a mentoring, coaching and psychotherapy practice that has witnessed these same matters coming up again and again with different people. These reflections are my way of speaking directly to you. They are to assist your thinking by, perhaps, providing an alternative viewpoint. They are not tutorials and they do not set out to tell you how to think. I hope that they stimulate and invigorate you – and intercede wherever you may have become jammed. I hope this will occur whether or not you agree with me. Reaching agreement is not the point. The point is for you to take a stance on how you see things. Too often we sit on the fence because we understand both sides of the story and, in so doing, do not learn to take a position. That's what these log entries are for me. This is the role they play. They represent the courage to take a position. Taking a position allows you to be actively engaged in the process of self-awareness and self-discovery. You will come to question how you think and what your beliefs are. You will become open to the many different viewpoints and perspectives that are out there. You will change your position when you do take one and, as you change, your consciousness will expand and so will your self-awareness. Is not one of the basic tenets of being creative the ability to see differently and from different perspectives?

The Creative Journey also offers activities to stimulate your mindbody. I use the term mindbody to refer to a holistic approach to activating your imagination through drawing, doodling, meditations and automatic and reflective writing. I have called these activities *Make Your Mark*. If you choose to engage in these exercises I would like you to get either a small art journal, one you can carry in your pocket – I love my pocket Moleskines, a 2B pencil and a very fine black or deep red felt-tip marker. If you feel a little more adventurous you can add a small pocket glue stick and a few watercolour pencils.

The *Make Your Mark* exercises are process-driven. They are not about producing great work; they are about developing your imagination. This goes hand in hand with embracing uncertainty. When you embark for the land of the imagination it may feel like you are wasting your time, that this is pointless and of no value except to entertain yourself or to pass the time when you are waiting for the train to arrive. Yet imagination is a gift that humans have. This gift is encouraged in our youth, but denied in adulthood. When we look at our planet, at great contributors of the past, like Einstein, Mother Teresa, Turner, Rumi and the many who inspire us today like Steve Jobs, Lady Gaga and J.K. Rowling, we do not only say that they are creative, we say that they are imaginative and have brilliant minds. Imagination is intelligence and intelligence without imagination is information.

For example, when we engage with the notion of doodling, traditionally we approach it as an activity with no underlying meaningful purpose. When we doodle intentionally we are instructing our mind to take the pencil and create random shapes in response to an inner feeling or a word. When we doodle with a mindbody approach our hand, heart and mind are taking a journey that is led by the pencil, the non-dominant hand and an open mind and heart. This doodle can be complete as it is or it can become the beginning of an artwork. This doodling may then become your own personal visual language, akin to Abstract Expressionism.

Either way, the process of doodling has accessed and brought out a subconscious part of you. Tapping into your subconscious is journeying into the unknown parts of yourself. This is where imagination loves to explore and this is where uncertainty surfaces and we question the validity of the process. When we engage in a new or different process, we connect with parts of ourselves that have been neglected and even excluded and this awakens and expands a different part of our brain. The brain has been called plastic. Neurological networks are created each time we try our hand at something new. We continue to build new pathways and to learn and develop fresh skills and flexibility in our thinking as we broaden our personal expression and invent. All this from doodling? Sounds a bit wild right? All of my *Make Your Mark* exercises are experiential. This means you need to experience them and then you can determine the benefits. It may be that the exercises prove an enjoyable respite, a distraction from your thoughts and a peace of mind. Or perhaps this doodle will open a passageway to a new painting or a chapter in your writing.

As you set out for Ithaka

hope the road is long,

full of adventures, full of knowledge.

Unfolding Your Personal Creative Process

You Have A Process

We are human beings who do. We do work. We do relationships. We do holidays. We do acts of kindness. We do art. We do decisions. We are always doing something and the way we do things is particular and peculiar to each and every one of us. That is what **Unfolding Your Personal Creative Process** is all about. I am introducing this topic at the start of this book because the five fact-finding steps that you take in a few pages' time will reveal things about yourself that you may not know. This means that you will continue reading this book having already experienced a personal shift and can fast-track your way to your greater creative self.

Unfolding Your Personal Creative Process is a five-step investigation to uncover your modus operandi. You do this by tracing out the steps you take in different scenarios to reveal what I am going to call your interior map. This map explores what is currently hidden behind your reactions, procrastinations and uncertainties and those non-trusting parts of what you do, when you try to process problems and challenges.

There is a great sense of freedom and fearlessness and faith in oneself when we understand our internal process. The thing is, we think we know what that process is but in fact we don't. We are not sufficiently conscious of the whole procedure, although we may be aware of parts, usually the yuck parts because they stick. By the way - don't discard these yuk parts. Messy as they might be they do bear gifts.

There is a template within you that carries you through a personal and creative process each and every time you want to achieve something. This template is your interior map. Knowing your interior map is a self-awareness process. It's about knowing how you act, what you think and what you do when you wish to achieve an outcome.

The interior map is not about the journey ahead; it's about the journey within. It is the way you move towards or pull away from an idea or a desire. You do this habitually, almost predictably.

It takes five short steps to uncover your personal creative process and create your own interior map. This interior map is made up of a series of points that record when you; procrastinate, deviate or doubt on your journey to Ithaka (your desired desti-nation), when you push away offers of help or expect things to come too quickly and easily and when you race through to get to the finish line regardless of the havoc you may be causing along the way.

Your interior map charts your unrecognised modus operandi. Are you aware that you have similar obstacles, concerns and expectations that cause you to move away from your goal or to even change course from something you really desire? We all have a way of getting things done, a way to resolve problems, but we may not realise that this is our own extraordinary process.

What is the first thing you do when you are faced with making a decision? What are the second and third things you do? This is what the map-making process will reveal to you in five steps.

Indeed, we may have several personal and creative processes that we operate from depending on the situation. For example, we may have a particular interior map that is triggered by things we fear, another which is activated when our reputation is under attack, a third when we feel unloved and yet another when we feel that we are just not good enough.

If we know how to cross the unknown territory that lies before us we can prepare ourselves and strengthen our resolve to go all the way notwithstanding the high waters and strong winds we encounter. It is an inner preparedness that I am referring to. This inner preparedness is a mindful process. It means that I can become mindful of how I react to the outer conditions. In fact instead of reacting I can learn to respond. When we learn to respond, we are making a conscious decision about the action we are taking. Reacting is unconscious – a knee-jerk response to external stimuli which we often regret afterwards.

Seeing this interior map spread open allows us to try to change the aspects of ourselves that we no longer wish to be controlled by. Or, where we can't make the change or choose not to make the change, to learn how to accept them in the best way possible.

How can we learn to accept these parts of ourselves? The best way that I know is through integration, which means that we allow them to become part of who we are. When we accept this, the journey becomes more enjoyable and we stop fighting our true nature and learn to love ourselves. By the way: don't be scared to love yourself. You are the only version of you, so why not? Love is an energetic force in unlimited supply. In my experience the more fearlessly you love, the more love boomerangs.

If the traditional map of the creative process was linear, it would have four phases: preparation, incubation, illumination and verification. But that is not what yours will necessarily look like. Your interior map is about capturing your personal creative process and appreciating its individuality. It may or may not follow any of the above phases, or it may follow all the above phases in a circular rather than linear manner.

In any case, the creative process is neither causal nor linear. It is not a series of logical steps that can be followed to secure a desired outcome. As useful as it is to learn about well-documented and researched variations, it is best to understand your own personal creative process – the one you already employ – because it's real.

Knowing how we see things, how we use language to explain, how we put ourselves down, allows us to identify the barriers that we have created, barriers that prevent us from taking risks and from having the courage to handle the outcome.

Making the interior map means that you will really see and understand your thoughts and your thought process and what you focus on. You will see where you become unstuck. You will know who or what you blame when things don't go your way. Your fundamental qualities will be revealed and your real personal strengths will outrun your imaginary ones! Yes, imaginary ones because we sometimes make believe what we would love others to see in us. This is one time when we use our imagination, imaginatively! When we do this it comes at a cost. The cost is getting to know our true strengths and growing them. Instead we try to strengthen our weaknesses. What happens? We become even. Our strengths that have not been grown become even with our weaker qualities that have been grown and well, we become what we think others want from us. And we become even. I would rather be myself, true to my nature, authentic as they say in current parlance and be considered odd.

At the end of the day, when you have created your interior map it will act like a fortune cookie: it will tell you what you will experience the next time you embark on a painting or any other form of creative expression or new project. When you know this, you have two choices: take the fortune offered by that cookie or grab another cookie!

Creating Your Interior Map

This is a dynamic process that I use with my students and clients over a period of five weeks. It has been a challenge to say the least to compress a dynamic, rigorous and interactive process into a two-dimensional written monologue. To enliven it for you, I have included interviews from people who have managed to make the whole journey. One of them wrote to me to say "I'd kinda lost the will to live by the last step, and that's where the juice is." I know that this sounds dramatic but it pretty much sums up the challenge that you will face with this process. It might also sound like I am not selling it to you, but I am! This person had completed the map in one go. That's so hard to do and I commend her for her tenacity. The best way is to take your time. Do Step 1 and then go and read another part of the book. Come back to it a few days later and continue. This way you will have given yourself the opportunity to allow the pause to work on you. The pause is similar to what happens when we sleep. The body heals during sleep. The mind loosens up when we pause and we don't get bogged down about completing the task. So take your time. Come and go from the map. One more last thought: even if you don't complete these five steps, reading about it and what others have said will prompt you to think about your own creative process.

Here we go:

There are five steps to this journey. They are simple steps, but they do require you to take them seriously. This requires time and contemplation. We are not easily persuaded to sit down and write out things about ourselves. I know what you're thinking: '*Why bother, I already know myself. I know what the outcome will be,*' etc. I want to encourage you to give this a go. I understand that we all believe that we already know ourselves, but I can guarantee you that it's a worthwhile process. When you write things down – like a simple list of things to do – writing them down changes your intent and your focus and things happen. I am asking you to write things down in this five step journey. You cannot look at the questions and listen to your responses in your head, they need to be written down. The process of writing will solidify and articulate your thinking. The process will change you because you will see yourself from a different perspective.

We think we know ourselves and there is nothing unusual about that statement. Ask anyone to tell you who they are and usually an occupation comes flying out. Then we may speak about our interests and our personal status.

This is an outward view of who we are. This is our exterior, our husk. The husk is not the seed. This process is about becoming aware of the core within you: your essence, your nature, that part of you that does not fluctuate or yo-yo or dither. Your core is where there is a certainty, a knowing. These five steps are gateways that open inwardly, the kind of journey that you may prefer not to take for fear you will find something you don't like.

This is the path of self-awareness, which you take to lose the idea of who you think you are and discover who you truly are. You may choose to focus on the better aspects of yourself once you know what they are and to work through the not-so-pretty parts – what we call in psychological terms your shadow. However I am jumping ahead. The first thing is 'know thyself'. Enter the white-bearded man wearing a toga called Socrates.

You may think that you do know yourself and that there will be no surprises if you take this five-step process. The thing is this, we have an *idea* of who we are, but that idea is rather a mythical creation. You catch a glimpse of it in phrases such as 'I am *always* on time', 'I *never* get angry', 'I am *not* judgemental' and other similarly absolute statements. We do have a strong idea of who we are and do not like it when someone contradicts it. We would not get so upset about other people's opinions if we were absolutely certain of who we are. Why? Because if you know that something is simply not true, you don't accept it. Who you are is not up for debate. Who you are is to be understood and you can't share that understanding with someone else if you yourself don't know who you are.

Are you ready to take this journey now?

You can continue reading this book. The choice is yours. You may want to come back to this section after you have read the journey musings or you may wish to give this exercise to someone else whom you feel needs it more than you do. Actually, I wish to encourage you to carry out these procedures because you cannot help anyone else if you have not first helped yourself.

| Step 1 The Story |

Recall a time in your life when you overcame a situation that initially overwhelmed you with fear, concern or uncertainty. It could be about something that you were duty bound to do or something you wanted to achieve.

I want you to recall what you experienced and how you felt and write down as much as possible about that experience and your feelings.

The topic can be anything. It can be about work, family, community or something to do with your art-making.

I would like you to write a minimum of 500 words, more if possible that describes the challenge you faced and how you felt. Then I want you to think about what it was that you did that got you through it? Reflecting on it now, what was it that surprised you? What was it that made you feel proud of yourself?

There is no wrong way to do these five steps. However you understand the instructions and however you respond, the process will still take you on a revealing inner journey.

You may benefit from seeing an example of responses. This is a response from RJ, one of my clients, to Step 1:

When I was 17 years old and completing my Higher School Certificate I chose to study Extension English and Visual Arts. For both subjects I was required to complete what was termed a 'major work' – a creative project on which I would be marked and which would determine a large percentage of my overall grade for the subject. For Extension English this meant writing a 10,000-word short story and for Visual Arts it meant the completion of a well-researched and resolved body of work.

When I first began the school year and was confronted with the idea of completing both projects, I felt overwhelmed. I was juggling all of my other subjects, as well as working in a part-time job after school and, like any 17-year-old, I had a lot of family and social commitments. I was also trying to apply for every university scholarship I could find, which meant I needed to complete a lot of extracurricular activities and earn an almost impossibly high UAI in order to present a compelling application. I was busy to say the least! But my main concern with my art and writing projects, was the idea of putting myself out there creatively. I was never short of ideas or inspiration. I knew exactly what I wanted to create – but for me the work felt extremely intimate, like laying bare the innermost workings of my mind and soul – and I was terrified of people witnessing these parts of myself. All of my creative ideas were heavily autobiographical and I felt vulnerable and nervous exposing so much of myself through my creativity. I worried constantly about what other people would think or say about my work, how they would look at me differently afterwards and how they would judge me.

For a while there I didn't know what to do. I would come home from school every day and, adhering to my carefully organised study schedule, I would sit down to write or paint. But I felt blocked each time I tried to create something. Every word I wrote, I would second-guess. Every mark I made with my paintbrush I would doubt.

But, because of the pressure of the HSC and the constant expectations being placed on me by my teachers and myself, I kept going. I had no other real option. I had always been a straight A student and, now more than ever, I needed to succeed and prove myself. At the time it really felt like my future depended on it.

Gradually I stumbled across techniques that helped me to loosen up and create. I realised that if I listened to music and really lost myself in it, I could paint without thinking. If I could get myself to stop thinking then I could stop judging myself. I would enter an almost trance-like state and just create. Likewise, I realised that if I listened to music and concentrated on the skill and poetry behind the lyrics, I would become inspired to write and could transform my emotional state so that I was in the right energetic state to do so.

Afterwards, I would look at what I had created and I would feel proud of myself. It was almost as though once it was out there I felt it was too late to take it back. I would accept what I had given birth to and the fear of the vulnerability it exposed me to evaporated. But the challenge was getting myself to take action – getting myself to do instead of to think.

I also realised that the busier I was the easier it was for me to work on these projects. At the start of the year I would sit there observing the time frame I had allocated myself for working on my art project or my writing, but nothing would really happen. Most of the time I just thought about what I wanted the end result to be. Or I mapped things out. I made lists and planned things in my mind. I daydreamed and visualised what I wanted to create and what the end result would look like.

But as the year wore on, I became busier and busier. Now when I sat down to write or paint there was a sense of calm frenzy. This had to happen. And now! I didn't have time to waste any more. I was regularly expected to show my teachers where my various projects were at and I had so many other commitments demanding my attention that it became a now or never situation. In such a crazy and hectic period of my life, writing and painting offered me moments of calm and refuge. I began to enjoy the process more than I ever had before. I saw my creative sessions as an escape and a chance to just be.

Before I knew it I had completed both projects. I handed them in and received higher marks on both projects than I would ever have imagined. My artworks were selected for an exhibition showcasing a selection of top HSC art students and I won a literacy prize for my writing.

In the end my grades were high enough that I was awarded a $30,000 scholarship to the university that had been my first choice and I was able to feel that I had secured the future that I had dreamed for myself.

Not only that, I felt truly proud of what I had created. My short story had explored my family's history and the stories interwoven throughout my life and those of my aunts and grandmother. When they read what I had written for the first time, they were overwhelmed and touched. As a family it was an experience that brought us closer together and bonded us.

I still struggle to allow myself to create fearlessly. Writing in particular is a struggle for me because it is the art form that calls to me the most. I still worry about how vulnerable and raw my writing makes me feel. But I feel called to do it nonetheless. And now when I do begin a new writing project, I know that I do have the ability to complete it. I have learnt that I do possess that strength. I just need to believe in myself and put in place strategies that support my own creative process.

| **Step 2 Forensics** |

Let's work with the information that you supplied in Step 1 and reconfigure it into three separate columns. In the first column you name the phase you were in. In the second column I would like you to describe the feelings you associate with this part of the story. In the third column list the words you would use to describe that phase. These are a series of single words that capture the quality, virtues, strengths and weakness of what you experienced. Basically we are stripping away the plot behind the story so that we are left with a series of phases and your emotional responses (second column) and what quality, virtues, strengths and weaknesses you associate with that emotional response (third column). A great tool to have handy for completing step 2 is a thesaurus. This is a reflective process and you will need all the tools you can gather. The best way to approach this section is to complete column one first, the phases of your story. Then you can choose to complete the third column and the second column in any order. Some find writing about emotions easier than finding what their corresponding qualities are and others have found that identifying their emotions challenged them more.

On the next page is RJ's response to Step 2:

Phases of your story	The emotions and behaviour you experienced	The way you described your phases
Beginning HSC and embarking on two new creative projects.	Excited, energized.	New, fresh, positive.
Starting to try to juggle my time and beginning to realise the commitment involved in delivering projects.	Overwhelmed, nervous.	Busy, confused.
Early phases of writing and painting.	Worried, feeling vulnerable and emotionally exposed.	Difficult, challenging.
Creatively blocked, but trying to make myself work each day.	Frustrated, felt as though I was not getting anywhere and all I was doing was procrastinating.	Stuck, determined, but confused.
Pressure point. Start to receive pressure from teachers and myself, start to worry about looming deadlines and running out of time.	Determined, new focus.	Motivated by fear and concern.
I work out processes and techniques that help me to get into the flow and I begin to create.	Relieved, re-energized.	In the zone, exploring ways to stay focused, brainstorming.
Phase of solid working and creating.	Satisfied, finishing each day with a sense of achievement and having accomplished something.	In the zone, exploring ways to stay focused, brainstorming.
Creative projects completed and submitted for marking.	Proud of myself.	Sense of completion and conclusion.
Results start to show. Receive good grades, positive feedback and opportunities, awarded scholarship, etc.	Exhilarated, excited, proud of myself, reminded of what I can achieve when I set my mind to it, newly confident.	Hard work begins to pay dividends.

| **Step 3 Rewriting The Story** |

What I would like you to do now is write a story that starts with 'When given a challenge, I generally…'

Use your findings from Step 2 (columns two and three) to write a general statement about how you resolve challenges. At this stage you don't have to believe it. I just need you to rewrite your story so it appears as a universally applicable approach towards life. When you have finished, read it out loud. How does it sound? Do you recognise yourself? This is your modus operandi, your interior map.

Here is RJ's response to Step 3:

When given a challenge I generally begin feeling very excited and enthusiastic. In the beginning I am full of ideas and am confident that I can achieve my goals and deliver on the project – for both myself and for anyone else involved. I feel elated and energised as though I am bouncing off the walls with excitement about what I am going to do, create, achieve. At this stage I have unwavering faith that everything will work out and that it will all happen. I am dismissive of anyone else's attempts to discredit my ideas or actions and am not easily dissuaded or discouraged.

I go into planning mode in my mind. I visualise the end result that I want to achieve and I work my way back from there, mentally mapping out what I need to do to get there. I make lists and think through all the minute details and form a plan.

After a fairly short period of time (sometimes a few days, sometimes a few weeks), I become overwhelmed and start to feel a bit flat. This usually comes just after my excited 'planning phase'. I realise how much time, energy, work and skill are required to achieve my goal and I begin to doubt myself. Whilst at the beginning I refused to see or acknowledge any potential obstacles or issues that needed to be worked through, now I worry that it is not going to be possible for me to achieve my goal due to lack of time or lack of talent or lack of resources. Now I become paralysed by all the issues that I can see.

For a while I feel frozen. Fear takes over. I am still thinking about the project constantly, but I find it hard to take action and begin to procrastinate constantly. I feel guilty that I am not doing anything or achieving anything.

This period can last quite a while. But eventually I start to put pressure on myself, which works in a positive way to move me to take action. Because I start to worry about not achieving my goals or impending deadlines or not being able to keep up with my peers, I begin to feel motivated to act. This motivation still comes from a place of fear, but I turn that fear into a positive and begin to feel energised again. I work out strategies and find tools that will help me to achieve my goal. I start to take action and enter a calm state of frenzied action. Things begin to move quickly and consistently. I become more and more determined and feel excited again by what it is I am achieving. I begin to believe in my initial vision again, but this time I have new clarity and understand better what I am doing.

Before I know it I have achieved my goal. Often this happens quite quickly. The longest part of my process is when I feel trapped in my phase of indecisiveness and inaction. Once I enter the final phase and begin to take action I find that I achieve results quite quickly.

When I have achieved my ultimate goal I feel proud of myself and a little amazed. I look back at all the things I worried about and I wonder why I let them get to me. I feel as though I have a new confidence and am reminded that I can achieve amazing things. I try to take note of the things I worried about and remember them for next time so that I can remind myself not to worry so much in the future. Or at least to find something new to worry about and not to worry about the same thing twice!

| Step 4 Backcast It |

Let's test your Step 3 interior map story. Quickly jot down another story from another part of your life. Select an experience where you once more overcame an overwhelming challenge. You can choose to write out the story fully or you can choose to simply jot down the story in bullet points.

Does the general statement that you wrote out in Step 3 i.e. your interior map, apply to this other situation? Is it similar? You can continue to test this out by 'backcasting' to other situations. Continue to think of and examine examples of times when you have been challenged and tweak your map in order to get closer to the way you process. You may find that you utilize several different processes, depending on the type of challenge you are facing. Or maybe it is always much the same process.

Compare and contrast the two (or more) stories and look for the patterns, similarities and differences.

The more you can articulate your process, the better you will begin to see what you wish to change or integrate into the overall way you respond to life's challenges.

Here is RJ's response to Step 4:

I chose to write out another story.

Between 21-25 I was in a committed relationship with a partner I loved. After four years, our relationship faced a serious challenge. My partner became very sick with mental illness and his life began to unravel. This was a devastating time for both of us and put a lot of pressure on our relationship.

At the beginning, when he was first diagnosed, I was strangely energised and almost felt excited. Finally, after months of uncertainty, we had a diagnosis. I thought 'now I can get to work and solve this! I can fix everything!' I was determined not to give up on him or our relationship and I went through a phase where I was constantly researching new ways of helping him and trying to take control of the situation, take action and fix things. I didn't realize that the power dynamic in our relationship had become untenable. I had voluntarily taken on complete responsibility for his wellbeing and was over-functioning – while he was increasingly under-functioning.

Eventually, when nothing changed and the positive results I had hoped for failed to show, I began to feel depressed. I kept trying and trying to control the situation, but there was nothing I could do to change things. I began feeling unhappy with the relationship and had a lot of doubts and fears about our future. I refused to acknowledge or admit these doubts to myself or to anyone else. I would constantly try to give myself pep talks and stay positive and believe that things would all work out.

For a long time, nearly two years, I was stuck in a place where I felt as though my life was on hold. I felt that I couldn't move forward and I couldn't move back. I was not taking any action because I was scared of what, deep down, I knew I needed to do. I was unwilling to face the reality of the situation and to admit that the relationship had hit an impasse, that it was over and that I no longer wanted to be in it.

Eventually, I had a light bulb moment. One day I saw a billboard in the city that said 'Things change when you change things'. I had a sudden realisation that the only thing I could control in this situation was whether or not I chose to stay. I had the choice to stay in the relationship, accepting the reality of the current situation and making peace with it. Or I had the choice to leave. Once I realised that, I finally admitted to myself that I wanted to leave. After that it was like being struck by a bolt of lightning. I felt energised again. I was nervous and scared about the changes that were taking place and I was worried and upset for the pain that my partner would feel during our break-up. But I was not as traumatised and upset as I had expected to be. I realised that subconsciously

I had already accepted that this needed to happen a long time ago. I had already mourned the end of the relationship without realising it.

Once I realised what I needed to do I felt a sense of urgency. I wanted my new life to begin as soon as possible. I felt relieved to be taking action and to be finally moving forward again. I went into a calm state of action. I took the steps that needed to be taken to gently end the relationship and then set about re-building my life again.

After a little bit of time and distance, I was able to feel relief that I had survived this tough experience. I was proud of myself for having the strength to pull through and to make the decisions that were right for me – even though at the time it had been hard and I had felt a lot of guilt. I felt a new sense of confidence and purpose. I realised I was much stronger than I thought. I also had a new appreciation and gratitude for life and for how blessed I was. I thought back over everything I had been through and tried to learn from the experience. I realised I had no regrets and would not have changed a thing, because I had grown and changed and learnt some valuable life lessons along the way. Those tough years made me who I am today and I am grateful for that.

To conclude this step of the process, I asked RJ to contrast the outcomes from both her stories and insights from her interior map. This is what she wrote:

Writing about my experiences, both personal and creative, has helped me to realise that my process does not vary that drastically… The general statement that I wrote out in step 3, does ring true and describe my process. There are subtle variations to how this process manifests, but when I look back and think about it, there are many instances in which I can see this process having underpinned a decision I've made or a journey I have taken.

When it comes to work or creative projects, I tend to be enthusiastic and excited but my downfall is the period of procrastination I experience. I allow myself to be paralysed by fear and in these instances that fear manifests as inaction. I become frozen – too scared to try to create – in case I fail.

I can see now that something very similar sometimes happens when I am faced with a personal challenge in my relationships. When faced with a significant challenge in a relationship, I freeze. At first I don't want to admit to myself that there is an issue and I don't like to face the reality of the issues and what needs to be overcome. I am paralysed again – but this time it is by worry. I become anxious and my thoughts tend to spiral. I am scared of what may happen and how things may change if I take the actions required. Eventually though, I realise that I need to take action and as soon as I make this decision I feel energised again. I begin to feel positive and optimistic about things and usually within a relatively short amount of time things will fall into place for me.

One of the key differences that marks how my personal process changes – depending on whether the situation is personal or creative – is where the motivation comes from that helps me to move forward. When it comes to my creative process, I am motivated by external factors: fear of not keeping up with my peers, by my competitive streak, by the belief and encouragement that my mentors and support network provide me with.

These are the things that push me to end the period of procrastination and to take action to create.

When it comes to my personal life, I am motivated to end periods of fear and worry by internal factors. For example, in my personal relationships, it doesn't matter what those around me think, or say, or advise me to do. I am very stubborn and I refuse to take action or deal with the situation until I am ready. I need time and space - and the motivation to finally change or take action always comes from within. I am motivated by my own realisation that something must change, not by any external influences.

Understanding and unravelling these patterns in my process has been incredibly insightful. I feel like I have learnt a lot about my own thinking patterns and feel better equipped now to change or work on the parts of my process that are holding me back.

| Step 5 Forecast it |

From Step 4 you will have seen your internal map highlight what you undergo as you navigate each journey. This particular process is either exactly the same or varies slightly depending on whether you are making a business decision, a personal decision, a relationship decision, a career decision or creating an artwork.

Until now you may not have realised that you have a pattern or understood that you experienced the same feelings, concerns and fears each time you embarked on a new journey, creative or personal.

Now we are going to forecast – we are going to contemplate the journey ahead. Forecasting is the final step and what you do is to map out what you expect to experience when you are contemplating a new project or about to embark on a new body of work or a career or relationship.

Have the steps from your interior map from Step 4 handy. On a clean sheet of paper name the project you are about to embark on. Follow your map from Step 4 and write out in greater detail what you expect to happen. In the previous example the first experience was feeling excited, energized and positive. Using this as a guide, I want you to flesh it out with a short narrative. If your new project is about a body of artwork then you might write something like this: I am about to embark on a new body of painting in encaustic work. I am excited because it has been two years since I last worked in the medium, so I want to find out if the materials or methods have changed. I shall be focused on this for several weeks and can see myself speaking to all my friends, artists and non-artists, about it. I may even enroll in a new encaustic workshop.

Once you have done this, you will either choose to accept the internal journey ahead or to change some part of it. Accepting it means that you will travel a little lighter and be confident about taking this journey. It's less about predicting what's up ahead, because that can and probably will change. The interior map is an awareness process and once you see yourself as a non-judgmental observer, not pronouncing on right or wrong you will merge with your true nature. At the end of the day there is no right or wrong way. There can be a frustrating way, a tiresome way or a burdensome way, but never a right or wrong. The simple act of observing ourselves is enough to make us kinder and less critical of our imperfections. The 'short and sweet' of this process is that you get to see how you think and how you feel. Seeing is the key word. It's not enough that you think that you know how you come to make decisions or what you imagine may be holding you back. When you see what you have written out on paper you may be surprised. Writing in itself facilitates a clarity that thinking in our heads does not. This is why other writing processes like keeping a diary are used in the therapeutic arts as well as in the creative arts to ignite the imagination. Writing is somatic thinking. It brings out the thoughts that keep cycling and recycling in our heads and allows us to look at what we have written and question the authenticity of our own thoughts.

On the next page is RJ's response to the final Step 5. This time it is a visual interior map, which can be completed relatively quickly.

My Interior Map for the book I will write...

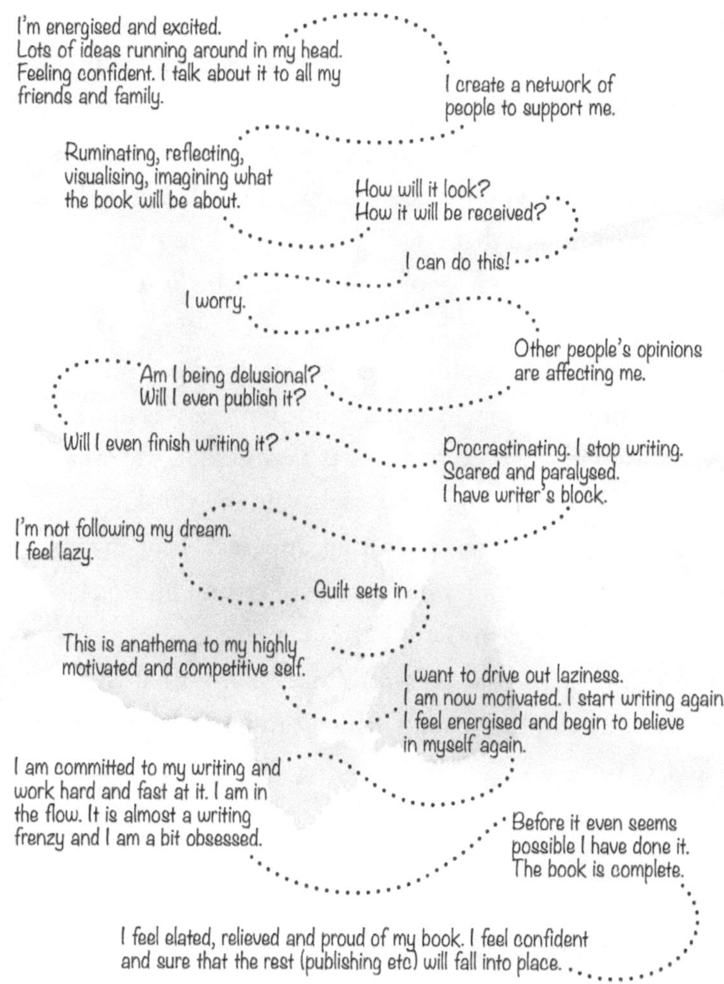

Interviews

The value of working through the interior map is best expressed by the many people who have already taken the journey. I interviewed four people who had completed the interior map exercise. The following is an interview with RJ, the person who completed the interior map for this book, which acts as a conclusion to appreciating the value in undertaking what might seem a gruelling task. Ah! But what you get on the other side of this has bewildered many of my students and they are all the better for it.

Interview with RJ

She is a manager in her late 20's.

Q. How did you feel about completing the Interior Map process?

Years ago I completed this exercise with Noula when I took one of her classes. I couldn't remember exactly what was involved in the process, but I remember at the time that it had a real impact on me and it definitely changed my attitude towards my own creative process. So I was excited to complete the Interior Map process again and see what I could learn from it... Having said that, I still felt a little daunted – it is hard to sit down and answer these questions about yourself. I found that if I completed one step at a time and then took a break before coming back to the next section it kept my mind clearer and made the process a lot easier. This process brings up a lot of thoughts and realisations and you need time to reflect before moving on to the next step!

Q. In what part of the process did you see a benefit and what was the benefit?

I felt the entire process was of great benefit! But Steps 3-5 were particularly beneficial for me. Having to really pull apart and break down the various phases of my own creative and decision-making process as part of Step 3 was really illuminating. It helped me to identify why I do certain things along the path of my creative process and when making a decision. Gaining this understanding helped in two ways. For example, I now feel less guilty about the fact that I procrastinate when working on a project. I now know and accept that this will inevitably happen. I can even predict when it is going to happen and have resigned myself without guilt to this being part of my process. Having said that, I am also working on reducing the time I spend in this procrastination phase and trying various techniques to keep me moving forward.

It was also really insightful to realise how my process affects my personal relationships and the decisions I make in my personal life. Realising that I do often enter into a phase of worry and anxiety was strangely empowering for me. I feel now that I can understand where the worry and anxiety has come from. I understand that it is just a reactive phase and that I can push through it. I think that next time I am experiencing this phase I will feel that I am able to acknowledge what is happening and make the decision to move through that phase faster and with more confidence.

Q. What part of the process was particularly challenging and why?

I found the second step to be the most challenging. Personally it was quite challenging to look at the story I had written and break it down into the various phases that make up my interior map. What I found challenging was trying to truly articulate the qualities of each phase of my experience and to separate these from the feelings or emotions I felt at each point. It made me realise that there is a distinct difference between what is actually happening at each phase of my creative process and how I am feeling emotionally. Once I realised this I felt that I could articulate my own journey much more clearly and therefore begin to take control of the direction in which I am headed, steering with more accuracy.

Q. What have you discovered about yourself?

I have realised that my biggest obstacle when trying to create something new or begin a new project is overcoming fear. I have plenty of enthusiasm initially and I have the determination and motivation to ultimately achieve my end goals. But I spend long stretches of time in the middle paralysed by fear. I end up wasting so much time procrastinating and therefore feel guilty that I am failing. For me this realisation has really helped, because now I understand that if I can just work on reducing the procrastination phase it will make a huge difference to how I do things! Having singled out the one thing I should work on and improve means I feel that I have a new clarity and new focus.

Likewise, I wasn't really aware previously of the phase of worry and anxiety that I often enter into when faced with a personal challenge. I experienced it! But I wasn't able to see it in a clearly defined way. Now I think I will be able to see that worry and anxiety coming. I will be able to recognise it and name it. I think that will help to defuse the power those emotions have over me and help me not to become so caught up in the moment.

Q. Has this insight had a positive or negative impact on you and how?

Definitely a positive impact! It has made me appreciate my strengths. I hadn't appreciated how determined I can be and I feel a new pride in being able to overcome obstacles such as fear and procrastination. It has also helped me to identify areas in which I want to improve. I want to be more willing to listen to others and accept the reality checks that are necessary in the earlier excited phases of an idea. Previously I have resisted people trying to point this out to me as I thought it was negative and it is important to me to try and have a positive attitude. Now I realise there is something to be gained from being more realistic and having a more rounded view of the situation – and that this doesn't mean I am being negative at all.

Q. In the last step I ask you to forecast. What did you get out of that?

Using my own interior map to forecast makes me feel more organised and prepared to take on a new project or journey. Knowing where I will stumble and where I will have difficulties allows me to plan ahead and arm myself with tools and strategies to help myself out when I hit these road bumps.

Q. Would you do the Interior Map again?

Absolutely! I would be interested in testing this out to see if I can work out the interior map that guides my personal relationships and how I make decisions, react and respond to someone I am in a close relationship with.

Interview with MF

She is in her early 50's, a businesswoman in the creative thinking industry and an artist.

Q. How did you feel about completing the Interior Map process?

I was curious to see what came of it - I love this sort of thing and am endlessly fascinated by creative processes in general and (obviously) my own in particular, so I was looking forward to the insights. I didn't expect it to take as long as it did or to be quite as intense. I did the whole thing in one hit - wouldn't recommend that approach to anyone else. I think it needs time in between the steps for your brain to process and for insights to bubble to the surface. In fact, my breakthrough didn't come out of the process itself, but from the sense that what I'd mapped didn't fit with an insight about my process I'd had a while back. When I put the two together and remapped it all, I had a huge 'aha!' which was brilliant.

Q. In what part of the process did you see a benefit and what was the benefit?

The biggest benefit for me was in the mapping, in the clarity of the awareness of how I work and what was useful, where I trip over and what the emotional cost is. This lets me reframe the tough bits that often lead me to abandon projects prematurely. I don't think I'm going to try to change my process, but I will change how I see and respond to the frustration and even mortification of over stretching and coming up short when I try new stuff. I'm hoping this will make me much more resilient and even encourage me to take more risks, knowing I'm likely to fall over but that that's okay.

Q. What part of the process was particularly challenging and why?

The final step, but I think that's because I did the whole exercise in one hit and was a bit over it by then. I probably need to go back and do that section again now that I've had a break from it. I suspect that instead of just trying to rewrite my emotional responses to an assumed series of project steps, that I'd now actually do a few different things and take a few more risks to get a bigger ROI (return of investment) from the inevitably painful bits.

Q. What have you discovered about yourself?

That the biggest thing that gets in my way are my expectations, and that the process I seem to have developed is really fast and works really well for me, but takes a lot of effort and cajoling to pull off without getting crushed. I've got two major areas where I derail myself - one at the beginning where my skills or resources fall way short of my enthusiasm and expectations (which feels like massive failure) and one later on when I get bored by the drudgery of getting the project finished. Hopefully now I can manage, reframe and use those periods better.

Q. Has this insight had a positive or negative impact on you and how?

Positive of course. Awareness always gives you more choice. I'm going to try to use that to get more of each experience, and to aim higher in terms of what I can tackle. And (hopefully) to be kinder to myself when I'm doing something new.

Q. In the last step I ask you to forecast. What did you get out of that?

See above. I need to do it again to see what happens. Hopefully this time I can run full tilt at the hard bits knowing I'm going to have to roll, so falling over won't hurt so much.

Q. Would you do the Interior Map again?

Yes, and differently. I have a different creative process in different contexts (e.g. working to someone else's brief vs. my own explorations and projects), so I want to map that and see how I can improve each from the other. I also want to see if I can use the forecasting part better. And I want to choose a couple of other stories to map to see how much variation there is and if there are more themes and insights I can use. But this time I'll do it over a few weeks rather than all at once.

Interview with LC

She is in her early 50s and an executive in the corporate world.

Q. How did you feel about completing the Interior Map process?

I was interested in what would come out of the mind mapping

exercise, and without having even started the exercises, I felt that I would probably need to ruminate on it some time afterwards for take outs or outcomes from it. Nonetheless I was very excited to try the process and see if I would have any "aha" moments as a result. I don't do sufficient internalising as I am a very task focused person, so I felt these exercises would force me to stop, take time out, internalise and ignite some emotional intelligence responses and insights.

Q. In what part of the process did you see a benefit and what was the benefit?

I struggled the most with step 2 in particular, in identifying the emotion and behaviour I experienced, and consequently I benefitted greatly from identifying these feelings. I often go into autopilot mode and I am so task focused that I can forget the emotional consequences on myself, those around me or on my project team, helping me to successfully pull off the task at hand. I also benefitted greatly from the backcasting and forecasting exercises as I could see a pattern emerging in which I can now accept that I will invariably go full throttle into projects with a plan A, but will invariably want optionality and a plan B to simultaneously work up as a failsafe. So as I appreciate this I know that I need to carry others with me on this, as it's not from a procrastination perspective but from a risk management perspective. It's also clear to me that I work best under pressure and have developed mechanisms to cope with this pressure. This insight will help me manage situations more proactively in future.

Q. What part of the process was particularly challenging and why?

I found the whole experience quite hard however I found part 2 to be the most challenging, as explained earlier. I go into auto-pilot-can-do mode and often do not take time out to analyse my feelings or emotions and it's clearly important to do so – not just for yourself but also those around you. It was very difficult to really pull apart each phase and to then describe the emotion and behaviour I experienced.

Q. What have you discovered about yourself?

I have discovered that although I am confident and I can tackle most challenges very successfully, I do have an innate fear that just once I might not be able to pull it off and it is this fear that drives me to my high expectations of myself and others. The whole process helped reinforce my understanding of what I already knew about my various traits and behaviour in many ways. Specifically what these exercises made me do was focus on my emotions and feelings and how they impacted on my behaviour, or vice-versa. I realise that my biggest hurdle is not wanting to fail in whatever I do, and having been very successful to date in my corporate roles, I clearly do not want to experience what failure is like. So it is important for me in my "corporate work mode" to take time out to reflect and slow down my autopilot task orientated self, so that any nervous energy or anxiety that I may be experiencing is not transferred to others or hinder my plans. I also need to balance things out more as my singular focus which helps give me clarity around a task can be quite confronting to others. As such I have learnt that I need to tone this down as necessary to bring others along with me. Whilst I work best under pressure, others around me may not and I need to be conscious of their work styles and feelings to maximize projected outcomes.

Q. Has this insight had a positive or negative impact on you and how?

This has to be positive as the more aware you are the more equipped you are to cope with given situations or experiences. What these exercises did for me was to delve into my responses and behaviour from an emotional intelligence perspective, which I know I do not do enough of, so in future I can try and use that knowledge in tackling similar situations.

Q. In the last step I ask you to forecast. What did you get out of that?

Knowing where I come astray is an amazing insight as it can help me plan and be more prepared in order to cope better next time around or even overcome those pitfalls altogether. Worse case, if I do not get the better of a new situation, I will know that I have coping mechanisms in place that will get me through it that time around as well. As noted previously, my biggest learning I believe is that having a singular focus may be counterproductive and to slow down the process, take the time out to reflect, and to use the forecast technique as a way of making that happen.

Q. Would you do the Interior Map again?

Definitely. I liked the visual nature of it, which really works for me, and I can certainly see it applying in various contexts. I am intrigued that if I do the mapping and forecasting process around different experiences, whether I will get the same points coming across as a pattern or whether different matters will come up for new insights.

Interview with GS

She is in her early 20s and starting out in her professional career.

Q. How did you feel about completing the Interior Map process?

It was a real challenge. Going in I didn't realise just how confronting and intense it would be. The actual task wasn't complex it was the regression and feeling all of the emotions once again that I face when originally confronted with the challenges I wrote about. The interior map clarified and organised my thoughts. As a person who finds it incredibly difficult to articulate their emotions I found writing exactly what I was thinking in a mind map, almost mindlessly created intense clarity. It took me almost a week to finish the whole process, I really needed breaks in-between as revisiting my challenges took an emotional toll, however the end result was certainly worth it.

Q. In what part of the process did you see a benefit and what was the benefit?

The whole process was beneficial, it taught me how to use hindsight as a tool in understanding and configuring my future. It also taught me some hard truths and created strong insight into how, why and what I do/have done when facing challenges.

Q. What part of the process was particularly challenging and why?

Regressing was the biggest challenge. I found it mentally draining and psychologically difficult to go back to challenging experiences, particularly the ones I chose, as they were quite personal matters. It was hard to feel those emotions as I had worked so hard to repress them for so long and re-visiting them made me re-evaluate the situations I had been in and draw links to earlier challenges of a similar vain. In saying this, repressing those emotions was clearly not the best idea as in the long run they sit, fester and eat away. This whole process made me realise how toxic suppression is and how important it is to understand your self, your tactics and how to harness hardship in cultivating greatness.

Q. What have you discovered about yourself?

I've discovered just how difficult I find it to articulate my emotions and this journey has really made it a lot easier for me to do so. My biggest obstacle when facing a challenge is trusting myself. I have great ideas, enthusiasm and plans however I become incredibly insecure throughout the process and worry that my ideas won't be good enough, well received, etc. This realisation has linked with so many (small) projects in the past that I have never overcome and has given me the faith and strength to revisit them and try to work through them again. Looking back on completed projects it became abundantly clear that the bigger and more important the project (usually non-personal projects) the more likely I am to follow through as I have external pressures such a deadlines and others relying on my completion of said task, it forces me to take the risk. Now that I know this is how I work it's allowed insight into why I struggle to follow through with my own smaller personal projects and has given me the tools to overcome this barrier.

Q. Has this insight had a positive or negative impact on you and how?

The overall impact has been a positive one, having my process down on paper allowed me to revisit and better understand my psyche in an organised coherent manner. It was a difficult task, I won't lie and it was psychologically exhausting, like anything worth having or doing it doesn't come easy. I've realised that putting things on the back burner to focus on more urgent matters is ok however, not to let these projects sit on the back burner forever, and to question why they're truly there in the first place. Am I avoiding or prioritising?

I've realised that my generally pragmatic and logical approach to projects and challenges can often be shrouded by emotional outbursts or suppressed emotional issues, such as not trusting myself or my fear of failure.

Q. In the last step I ask you to forecast. What did you get out of that?
Forecasting creates a visual journey. For me, being able to see my process clearly and visually gives me to the tools to prepare for future projects, what my obstacles will be and how to overcome them. I feel like I'm facing projects with success in mind, not walking blindly.

Q. Would you do the Interior Map again?
100% I used the process on both workplace and personal challenges which created a polarity between the two different ways I deal with challenges. This is certainly something I'll be using when I hit a stalemate with any future projects, or even just as a means of checking in with myself.

Always keep Ithaka in your mind.

Arriving there is what you are destined for.

But do not hurry the journey at all.

Better it lasts many years;

and you arrive an old man on the island.

The
Quest

Quest?

Have we lost the art of dialogue, the art of exchanging ideas and viewpoints? It seems that instead of wishing to participate in an exchange of ideas, theories and perspectives, we are seeking instead to change the other's viewpoint. Have we become attached to being right? Or maybe we don't like being wrong? In my psychotherapy practice, I often get to hear couples talking. Each person becomes defensive about their ideas and thoughts and their general outlook on life. They are not seeking to understand, they just want the other person to know that they are in the wrong.

How can we learn to experience the wonder of a true exchange of viewpoints, life experiences and reflections, where the acts of giving and receiving are inclusive, where there is no right or wrong, but just is? For in this 'just is' place, insights and things we didn't see before will naturally come to light. This is Quest, a space where we explore each other's questions and renounce the need for answers, where giving and receiving encourages our imagination and we enter a place of wonderment. The power of Quest is the way in which our imagination is prompted through the simple process of an interchange of questions, where powerful, infinite insights take the place of narrow, right answers.

Quest is the art of questioning and suspending the need to pursue an answer. It is an art because there is no predetermined answer, consideration and contemplation. It requires you to search for the most fitting words as you form the question. It demands articulacy. It obliges you to engage with your imagination. It forces you to make things up in the creation of a question. These are the nuances of Questing, like searching for the most compelling tone or colour for your painting, or the most alluring movement in a line drawing - nuances that are simple yet which express so much.

| How To Quest |

Two people are necessary to Quest. You need a piece of paper, a pen and silence as well as a genuine and enquiring attitude with which to pursue each other's questions. One person begins by writing a question down on a piece of paper. The other person responds to the question with another question on the same sheet. I usually Quest for 10 questions in total or until five questions have been asked by each participant. But then again I once Quested for 90 minutes non-stop with one person. I have included a section at the end of the Quest transcripts where you too can Quest with a friend.

| The History Of Quest |

This book exists partly because of my public art performance called Quest. Because several hundred people sat down to engage with me silently around a colourful piece of blotted paper. Because since 2011 I have transcribed over 6,000 questions and I wondered what all this meant.

Was it as simple as that? In some ways, yes! Why did so many people want to exchange 10 questions with me? At a practical level, the attraction is its simplicity (not much instruction required), spontaneity (no one knew where the dialogue would go) and the short time frame required (in our current time-poor society, 10 questions seemed feasible).

I have learnt that Quest engages with the imagination to uncover what is really on our minds when we ask a question. Most of the time we say one thing but mean another and we expect the person we are talking to to be able to grasp what we mean automatically. Both parties get frustrated and then we end up saying "You don't understand me." What's closer to the truth is "I just don't understand my Self." The reason why this happens so often is that, contrary to our faith in a dictionary, all words that are used to describe or explain are subjective. We impose our own meaning on words or we come to our own conclusions, conclusions that are not even based on experience. For example we may say "I can't draw" without ever having tried to learn.

Quest is a way of getting to know ourselves better. In a sense it is a self-awareness tool. Its simplicity and child's play approach allows the imagination to be engaged. Imagination is the welcoming committee for insight.

I created my public performance art Quest from my coaching and psychotherapy practice. I had been coaching clients for a while – some were artists, others young managers and many were career managers and executives. Although I am an artist and a psychotherapist, I previously had an 18-year career in the corporate world. I understand the environment of the workplace and its pressures, the desire to realise our ambitions in the workplace and balance them with a personal life. How do you create harmony between personal and professional goals? Will they always be incompatible?

When I am coaching I make no assumptions. This means that I ask a lot of questions. By the time the client and I have explored the topic that has been presented, the client has a deeper understanding of their concern. At this point I may ask a series of provocative questions to inspire their imagination to look from another perspective. This other vantage point I call 'over there' and I ask my clients "What do you see?" As a coach/therapist, I don't know what's over there – but I do believe in there being an 'over there'. This is how I embrace uncertainty. 'Over there' is unknown and the best tools we have to explore it are our imagination and curiosity.

Having experienced being coached by me, my gallery curator asked if I would turn what I do in my therapeutic practice into an exhibition, a performance art exhibition. What? No sculptures, no drawings? What's performance art anyway – is that a real art form? An instant later I said "Yes, absolutely!" There was no vision, just a feeling that this was a direction worth exploring. After all, everything I do is interconnected. This exhibition could explore that interconnectedness.

Within a few days I had found large sheets of watercolour paper that I would drip paint onto and watch it slide down. I would then spray on water and add other media and more colour. Each artwork in turn gave birth to a new work as I created monoprints like the psychological mirror images of Rorschach, the inkblot test images used to stimulate the subconscious. 'That's interesting', I thought, 'the inkblot test!' So is it possible that people participating in this exercise would spend time selecting the design on the paper they wanted to Quest on? Apparently so.

I have performed Quest in public spaces, company settings, art fairs in Sydney and Melbourne and via Skype, with universities and in art galleries. Generally each iteration of Quest is an endurance performance. The longest was four days of seven to nine hours a day without a break. I performed at the Sydney Contemporary Art Fair in September 2013 and at the Melbourne Contemporary Art Fair in August 2014. I set up a space that had pink infused lighting. I sat on a carpeted floor with oversized cushions, a wooden table in front of me, coloured pens and pencils and ink-blotched papers. When someone arrived, they sat opposite me in silence. No words were exchanged. The guest selected a sheet of coloured paper and wrote their first question. This was handed to me so I could respond with another question. And so the written interchange continued in silence for the duration of five questions each, culminating in a total of 10 written questions. I have now collected over 6,000 questions. The Quest transcripts and video footage of the performances can be viewed at www.noulaquesting.blogspot.com.au

Questions beginning with why are not always seeking answers. They are seeking to be soothed mostly. My client Ann asked why she is fat. I asked if she wants to lose weight. She said of course she does. I asked if she knows how to lose weight. She said none of the diets that she had tried worked and that she had tried all of them.

"Is it the diet that doesn't work or is it you on a diet that doesn't work?" I asked.

Ann looked at me and said "I see. It's me, right?" I asked her to ask me another question.

It took about five minutes for her to respond with "How can I get healthy?"

That is a very different question to her original "Why am I fat?" question.

Other 'why' type questions can lead into wonderment and arouse our curiosity, because they are at the opposite end of the spectrum. Knowing the answer doesn't make the question any less intriguing because there is still something mysterious behind the answer that informs us.

For example:

Why does the rainbow always show the same seven colours in the same order?

Why do leaves change colour?

Why do we have a fever when we have an infection?

And other questions are those of deeply held and painful personal beliefs that are seeking to be met with compassion.

Why don't you love me?

Why can't I do well in interviews?

Questing makes us think differently about what we think our dilemma is, what we think we are puzzled by and brings us to realise what deeply concerns us.

How to develop better questions is what results from Questing. Better questions are ones that help us realise what we are truly seeking to understand. Because you get to ask question after question without answers, you scramble through your brain to find alternative words (not necessarily synonyms) that align more closely with what you sense or feel about something because the continual questions cause something to crack. Eventually the intellect relaxes, emotions start to surface and you begin to uncover the 'not quite right-ness' that was sitting behind the original question. The insight is revealed in the form of a better question. One that can drive a solution and away from feeling distressed.

At the end of the day, there is no one right answer when it comes to looking for a response to our personal challenges. What we want is that feeling that this is the right way for me right now.

We all have different perceptions of reality. We may all witness the same event, yet each description of it will differ. Our need to be understood has been usurped by the need to be right and have that need for rightness affirmed. If we let go of the need to be right, then we can let go of the need to convince others to agree with us and focus instead on being understood. That is the power of Questing.

| Transcripts From Quest |

These are transcripts of Quest that I have documented from my performance art with people from the public that chose to sit with me. Some of these transcripts date back to the very first performance in 2011. I have not made any grammatical corrections. They are transcribed exactly as they were written. There was no particular topic that was barred from discussion and there was no particular topic that a participant had to write about. I decided to group Quests of a similar theme and the results have taken me on another journey.

There are many pauses, long and short, that the participants and I experience during Questing. These pauses are unexpected by participants who imagined an exercise of 10 short questions would take no time at all. Of course it's not about how long the question takes to be written, it's about how long it takes to create. And in that pause of creativity, a subtle mental and emotional shift is experienced and we both become engrossed in an intimate interchange regardless of being strangers to each other.

Expressing a feeling takes time to translate into words and this becomes paramount in Quest for that's all we have. Written words. The written question cannot be augmented by talking it through. Quest is experienced in silence. When you read these Quests, I would ask you to also pause after each question. Just for a moment. Take a breath. Imagine that you are Questing with me. Imagine that you are asking me the question. That small pause will help you to experience the depth that was reached between me and the other person. I would prefer you to snack through these Quests rather than gorge yourself with them all at once like the intake of fast food. Take your time. Enjoy the experience. Allow yourself to wonder does this Quest apply to you? What question would you have asked in response? Engage with the interchange of Quest.

In all the following transcripts of Quest, the questors' questions are in bold and mine are not.

| Quests About - What Does It Mean To Be Human? |

Even though we all share the same experiences and are all part of what we call the human race, I often wonder what we really know about oursel.

Know thyself. This famous maxim has been attributed to several Ancient Greek philosophers, most notably Socrates, and was engraved on the Temple of Apollo at Delphi, where Greeks would go to ask questions, hoping to receive guidance from the priestess of the Oracle. The same search to know ourselves continues today as we read self-help books, look for explanations in science and religion and go to counsellors, psychologists and psychiatrists in the hope of understanding how our minds work and what makes us who we are. One of the core techniques of counsellors is, perhaps unsurprisingly, a version of the Socratic method.

Essentially, in seeking to know ourselves we must question ourselves or at least be open to considering questions put to us.

By asking questions we become aware of things that may not have occurred to us before. And without asking a question, how could we ever find an answer?

By seeing some of the questions that other people ask of themselves and of humanity, perhaps some questions will come to you that will open a new path of thought and questioning.

What does it mean to be human?

Which aspect shall we discuss, physical, emotional, mental or spiritual?

Are all the above linked in ways that cannot be separated and defined individually?

Is that what makes us human?

Does this mean that other life forms fail to display a similar kind of 'oneness'?

Does oneness require consciousness to be experienced?

How do we define or how do we know, whether a being is conscious?

What is the process of awareness that accesses states of consciousness?

Does this mean that all beings have multiple states of consciousness, but it is the awareness that sets one apart from the rest?

Reflection

There were many reflective pauses, staring into the void and searching within before a response was given. I recall that there was a stillness enveloping us. The questions are odd and this strangeness is what makes Questing interesting. It ignites our imagination to make sense of the question. Our imagination catapults our thinking, allowing us to speculate, to fascinate and to suspend what we initially believed to be our position, our answer.

How does one know when to stop?

Do you wish to stop or do you wish to pause?

Do you continue with negativity?

Does negativity expand or contract you?

What does a colour mean to you?

How does the universe want us to see that we are alive?

Are all colours the same at one level?

Can we see all the universe's colours?

Are colours interpretations by us, just like religion and everything else?

And are some people colour-blind?

Is that good or bad?

Can we love them anyway?

Reflection

Why does something have to be either good or bad? I understand that we want to explore our options, to make the best decision we can. However to explore all experiences through the lens of good/bad thinking takes away the opportunity to look at the topic at hand as it is – without judging it. This generally means that we are seeking to fit into an 'either/or' box – a good box or a bad box – and once we have labelled something this way then we end up applying the same reasoning to other similar topics. That's why I concluded this Quest with the question "Can we love them anyway?"

Am I good enough?
Is it enough to be good?
Why am I here?
Do you want to go back?
How am I here?
How are you, you?

Reflection

These questions capture so much about the way we examine ourselves and the way we seek meaning and purpose. There was an immediate shift in the Questor's demeanour when she read my response to her first question "Am I good enough?" Then I experienced an internal adjustment when I wrote the final question "How are you, you?" I now prefer to use this last question with clients, in place of "Who are you?"

Where does it go?
Is comfort an attitude?
Is pain real?
Are you referring to emotional or physical pain?
Are they different?
Are there different parts of us that therefore manifest differently and, if so, do we treat them differently?

Are you Buddhist?

Do you recognise me?

Are we looking for ourselves reflected in our friends?

Do you require intent to 'look' and then awareness to 'see'?

Is truly seeing someone else, and therefore maybe seeing ourselves, an uncomfortable experience?

Reflection

An odd start to this Quest and I sat with the first question for a while and began to feel uncomfortable, which led me to my response question "Is comfort an attitude?" The Quest became one of seeing – another word is awareness – and what that means. I didn't end this particular Quest. Usually I write the last question. Curiously, the question that it ended on returned to my first response question about comfort!

How can I get more balance into my life?

How have you already got balance?

I don't have enough and I'm wondering why?

Is there more than one kind of balance?

Isn't there more than one kind of balance?

What does balance mean?

Not cramming and rushing, what do you think?

What does my definition matter to your life?

So much revolves around what other people think, don't you agree?

Why don't you mind your own business?

I have another question, how can I listen more effectively?

Do you know how to keep your mouth closed when you dive under water?

Is that possible?

Do you know how to drown?

Reflection

The idea that we have a balanced life but want more equilibrium – is that possible? You are either level-headed or not. The scales are counter-balanced or they are not. If you want more stability then must you not also want more imbalance just so the equation cancels itself out?

My last question went to a dark place. "Do you know how to drown?" If we have allowed ourselves to fail in life, then we have also had the experience of dealing with failure. When we do, we discover qualities and strengths that we may not have known about before.

How can I learn to be more calm at all times?

Do you want to be calm at all times?

No, how can I learn to remain calm during moments of stress or disagreement?

Is stress the same as disagreement?

How do I learn to walk away from disagreements feeling happy and proud of how I have handled them, rather than disappointed?

Are you disappointed in yourself or are you disappointed because the other person appears disappointed?

Should I be disappointed in myself or do I just need to learn to be kinder to myself?

Are you minding your own business?

Reflection

Whom do we get upset with when we encounter an unwanted outcome? Many times we choose to blame someone else. And while this may make us feel good because 'it's not my fault it's their fault', then what do we do? We cannot change anyone else. But we can change how we choose to respond. That's empowering. Hence my last question "Are you minding your own business?" suggesting that we spend more time minding other people's business than our own, telling them what they should and shouldn't do so that we can feel better about ourselves. What if we turn this statement towards ourselves?

Am I really here?

Who am 'I'?

Does 'I' matter?

How would 'I' feel if 'I' didn't matter?

How does it feel to be 'I'?

How would 'I' know?

Would you like to be 'I'?

Could I be anyone else other than 'I'?

If 'I' became 'we', would 'I' be lost?

How many 'I's does it take to become a 'we'?

Could we be two single 'I's?

Does it take two to tango?

Can I dance forever?

Reflection

I am smiling as I reread this Quest. It can be interpreted in so many ways, which is also part of the pleasure of Questing. It's fun for the two people who are Questing and it's interesting to read someone else's Quest. You simply need to read them slowly, for they were written slowly. So read them as if you were overhearing two people's conversation… because it is a conversation.

What is the world coming to?

Is the world coming or going?

Are some aspects coming and some going?

Is this something like to-ing and fro-ing?

Does it matter?

What is matter?

Is the world matter?

Does the world matter?

What is the world that it should matter?

And if it weren't matter, what would the world be?

Would the world be you and me?

If we are the world, what is everyone else?

Are they all that matter?

Mmmm… does it matter?

Is matter what the world is coming to?

Ah – what's the matter with you?

Reflection

Of course you can Quest and play with words like this Quest. Yet there is something quite curious evolving from the way the word 'matter' has been used throughout this Quest. And now I am wondering if an idea is matter? Is it?

Is a self-portraiture narcissistic?

Is putting make-up on narcissistic?

Is one's face meant to be shared with the universe?

Do you like wearing masks?

Do you?

Do you find masks comfortable?

Have you ever seen me in a mask?

Can we see more than we are shown?

Do we want to show more than we can see?

Do we want to be told more than we know?

Who doesn't?

Does everyone have faith?

Is our time up yet?

What is time and how is it measured?

How do you find the courage to draw across the face when all the rest has been around it?

Reflection

A number of my Quests are written on paper that I have splashed with ink. One sheet had an abstract face on it and the person who was Questing with me wrote in a circle around the image. I just wrote across it, which prompted the last question. It was interesting that the Quest was about masks and faces and self-portraiture, which might have been prompted by the ink-splashes on this particular Quest paper where an abstract face appeared. But when I wrote over the face the other Questor was alarmed and thought I needed courage to do that, whereas it was not an act of courage at all…

| Quests About - Am I Creative? |

Of course everyone is creative and that is what this book is all about. I say this with confidence because I have yet to meet someone who has come away from my class believing that they are not creative.

Have I met people who believe that there is not a creative bone in their body? Yes. I have met many people who believe that they are not creative. I meet them in every single one of my art classes. I meet them at art exhibitions. I meet them when I am out shopping and in social gatherings.

Of course there are many people who have convinced themselves that they are not creative. But I don't believe them because I don't agree with their definition of creativity. There is an assumption that people who believe themselves to be non-creative make and that is, to be creative you must have artistic skills, be capable of drawing amazing realistic representations of the world, be born with talent and have the ability to intuitively create works of beauty. How do you define creativity?

Am I creative?

What does it mean to be creative?

How do I know if I'm creative?

Who defines creativity?

Is it okay to be creative?

Is there any other way to be?

How can you truly, honestly and deeply explore your creativity?

Does it begin with having the courage to be authentic, whatever that may be?

How do you know which door to unlock and how to unlock the door itself?

Do you think that we should focus on why you want to open the door first of all and then the how and the which will follow later?

Reflection

I find these questions singularly interesting. Each one on its own reveals something about our hesitancy, perhaps even our fear, to explore creativity. I wonder for example about the question "Is it okay to be creative?" Why would it not be okay and what would make creativity not okay? Is it because you cannot make a living out of creativity? Fair enough, but is that the only reason why we say we are not creative? Can we not be creative in all the other parts of our life?

What made you choose mosaics as your medium?

Does the medium choose you or do you choose the medium?

If you choose the medium, do you ever feel limited by it? Or does it inspire you further to go deeper?

Is that a matter of attitude – being one thing that I can choose?

How can you find inspiration in the little things in life and then translate that into little pieces of glass glued onto a canvas?

Is imagination like a magnifying glass that allows us to delve and then see subtle things?

How can I create such imaginative pieces, like you?

Do we each have our own individual voice that it is up to us to discover, explore and then accept and allow to grow?

Do you learn new techniques by experimentation?

Is life a series of experiments that create our wisdom?

If life is a series of experiments, then what is your hypothesis?

Can I have more than one and can they contradict each other?

Reflection

This Quest is a classic art-meets-life Quest. Because of this coincidence (a coincidence is where two points meet and fit perfectly together), my art classes, personal growth classes and this book all come together beautifully. This particular Quest is easily followed because there are references to an answer within the question. You may wonder why not just answer the question? Because no one likes being told how to think or what to do. Humans are explorers. We want to find out for ourselves along the way. We love master guides and co-travellers, but we don't like being bossed.

How would you handle the uncertainty of not knowing which season came next?

Is change an opportunity for growth?

Are growth and change worthy of their inhabitants?

Is our journey to discover our worth through change?

Will the journey be only for those who can grasp its intent?

Is intent to be grasped or do we create it?

Does creation have the opportunity to grasp and change?

Who creates?

Who does not?

Do some of us think/believe that we cannot create?

Do social limitations stop us creating?

Why do we obey perceived social rules and limitations?

Is it that we are scared of what we cannot label?

Reflection

More pauses are needed to engage with this Quest. The content is reflective and should make us meditate deeply as we read it. I like the last question the participant raised. If you think about it, it also links back to the first question.

The first question was a matter of being uncomfortable about something we have always known appearing in the wrong sequence. This would be a leap into the unknown. Would there be a different order of seasons or would they fall randomly each year? How would nature react? The final question suggests that we fear what we cannot categorise.

Why make art?
Is art made or created?
What is the difference?
Are we a maker or creator?
What have we created, and what is made?
Is making the process for creation?
Is one contingent on the other?
Is an idea made or created?
Is art made or created?
What is art?
What is anything?
Is life art?
When and where is life?
Does life have an address?
Is it where and when you make or create it?
If it is, how would I contact life?

Reflection

Two curious questions here, "Why make art?" and "What is art?" have an enduring and puzzling effect on me. I am still exploring these questions with artists and my students. My journey into the world of reflective writing was in part governed by these questions. I guess I will leave them to marinate and reappear in my second book!

What are we doing here?
Does everyone do?
How do we know we should be here?
If we were not here where would we be?
If I were somewhere else, how would I know where I should be?
Do you only belong in one place?
Can I be in more than one place?
Do you have an imagination?
Am I my imagination?
Have you created yourself?
Can I create somebody else?
Is it possible to recreate yourself?
Can we change by using imagination?
If we don't use imagination to change ourselves, do you think we leave ourselves open to other things changing us?
Who else can change us?
What else can change us?

Reflection

Questing on the role of the imagination has led me to think about how external events and people have often contributed to the idea of 'who I am' more significantly than my own subjective research. It's easy to track and to rationalise how I got to be where I am today. But what part of me today is authentic? What part of me have I authored? Who is the author of me anyway?

How do you know if your creativity is being limited by your work surroundings?

Can anything stifle your creativity?

Is there a point in time where your external passion tells you that it's time to move on, at the expense of job security and certainty?

Is there truly anything that is certain in life and if there was, why would anyone want it?

Do you believe that things happen for a reason?

Are you here 'on purpose'?

Is it that the purpose or reason is known to us, and that we just choose to ignore it or put it off?

If we are born 'on purpose', is our journey to discover/uncover it and then to have the courage to pursue it?

What is true courage as opposed to the definition we think it is?

Does courage mean facing your fear or does it mean absence of fear and does one definition feel more courageous than the other?

Can courage at times be a definition of convenience for the given circumstance and can courage defined incorrectly be stupidity for that decision?

Reflection

My favourite question was "What is true courage as opposed to the definition we think it is?" This kind of question brings Quest to the heart of the matter. What do we understand of the words we use? The etymology of the word courage comes from the word heart. Courage doesn't mean fearless. If it did then its core meaning would become heartless. Courage means to take heart and do it anyway.

| **Quests About - What Is Happiness?** |

We are forever seeking to be happy, to find ways that will allow us to experience the state of happiness and to avoid sadness at all costs. We say we will be happy once the mortgage is paid or the children have grown up or when we have met our other half. Why delay happiness? Why wait for something to happen before we can be joyful? There are many examples, mostly from the research files of positive psychology, that show how happiness ensues when we love what we do. Happiness therefore is not something to be pursued as an outcome. We rely on others for our happiness, on the economy for our happiness, on the weather for our happiness. My mum suffered from fibromyalgia. This did not stop her from feeling joy. Nor did it not stop her from being grateful. She found ways to manage the crippling pain syndrome that fibromyalgia is. This doesn't mean she was laughing and joking all the time. Not at all. At her darkest times, when the pain became unbearable, she would withdraw. I could see it in her eyes. I would know how to be there for her when I witnessed her in this condition. I kept silent; I played meditative music and we both waited holding hands, but sometimes even that was too much. She never spoke to us about her illness and she didn't allow it to define her. This is reminiscent of Victor Frankl's book '*Man's Search For Meaning*'. A holocaust survivor, he would bless the fish-bones floating in his water soup before eating.

What is happiness?

Is it something different for everyone?

Does this mean there are many different types of happiness?

Does that feel exciting to you?

Could the same thing make some people happy and other people unhappy?

Should we adopt a philosophy of live and let live?

Is excitement a fundamental ingredient for happiness?

Or is excitement one of many outcomes of happiness?

Could it be both?

Would it limit our experience of happiness if we depended on both?

Does everyone strive for happiness?

Is avoiding pain the same as striving for happiness?

Are people happier if they have experienced pain in the past?

Is gratitude the same as happiness?

Maybe happiness is an elimination of difficult experiences?

Reflection

I spent some time reflecting on whether people are happier if they have experienced pain. Our capacity for compassion can only be derived from our own suffering, otherwise we feel pity. Compassion and empathy are not pity and no one wants to be pitied. If someone pitied me I would feel rejected, an outcast. I would feel marginalised and not part of the human race. I would feel leper-like. But when someone can sit with my pain and hear me and not try to fix anything, well, that's powerful.

What is success in life?
Can there be more than one definition of success?
How do I manage the competing priorities to feel successful?
What are your priorities competing against?
How do I plan my day or week to give all my priorities enough 'air time'?
Is it a question of time or is it a question of energy?
Can women have a mid-life crisis?
Are we given the gift of crisis so that we may grow?
Does growth lead me on my journey to 'success'?
Can success be defined as having the courage to take the journey?

Reflection

This Quest was beautiful and rereading it made me feel successful. I like my last question and if I write it out as a statement it reads 'success is having the courage to take the journey'. Like anyone who embarks on something new and unknown, success is defined by being willing to get on that ride and hold on. Enjoying it too would be a bonus!

Why do I feel so stressed?

What does stress feel like?

What should it feel like?

Can stress be positive?

Does it need to be positive?

If stress is negative, does it serve you in anyway?

In what way could it be of service?

Can stress act as a reminder that there is something requiring attention and possibly change?

So would making changes really fix stress or is it engraved in one's DNA?

Is DNA fixed?

Isn't life direction pre-determined by fate?

Who deals the cards?

Do you think I could reject that hand and start a new one at my own selection?

Do you have an imagination?

Do you need imagination or could you use facts available?

How will you use the facts with or without imagination?

Reflection

The opening question has come up in many Quests held in corporate settings. However this particular question wasn't about how to deal with stress it was that they didn't know why they felt stressed. I think this is true for many of us when we have feelings that we don't understand. We don't always understand why we get upset, angry, frustrated and other similar feelings. Usually we try to rationalise the feelings by blaming someone else for making us feel that way. But is that true? If stress is in our DNA why do we blame others?

Why do we spend so much of our time worrying?
What is there to worry about?
Why do we think about those things over which we can't control?
What part of us wants to control things?
Is our mind telling us that we should have more balance?
Are we using 'control' to create balance and if so, are there other tools?
Can we 'control'? What is that?
Are we trying to control 'things' external to us, wanting something outside of us to be different?
If that is the case, how do we change our direction and thoughts?
How can we learn to mind and be mindful of our own business?
Do we have to mind our own business if we are trying to make a change in direction?
Can the only true thing we can change be ourselves, and if we pursued this and created the best of what we could be and presented that to the world, would that create a change in direction?
What happens when a change in direction requires not only a change in one's self, but also the desire for change in someone else?

Reflection

This is the perennial belief that if others fix themselves then we would be happier because we are perfect. Why do we want others to change? Our happiness is not the responsibility of others. Is it?

What makes you happy?

Is it different to what makes you happy?

Does happy mean different things to different people?

Is that why we have wars?

Or does conflict e.g. war help us realise what happiness is?

Is it hard to make everyone happy?

Is it our natural state to be happy?

How do we maintain our natural state?

Do we want to maintain our natural state?

Would it be false not to?

What is truth?

Is seeking our truth, our essence that brings us happiness?

If we spend our whole lives seeking truth, does that mean we never experience true happiness until the end?

Can the journey, being on path, and that alone, bring a state of happiness, or is happiness a destination?

Is happiness a state we can control with our thoughts or an emotion, fleeting?

Reflection

Defining what personal happiness is and the suggestion that the definition changes when we talk about global happiness and the idea that they may always remain separate and unable to be integrated, intrigued me. Is it because we are all seeking to agree on one definition of happiness? The questions get bigger. They are matters of morals and ethics, about what's right and what's wrong at a humanitarian level. Sometimes we forget that humans make up humanity.

| **Quests About - Relationships** |

Everything on this planet is in a relationship. I am in relationship with my family, my neighbours, my community, my planet, my Self, my higher Self and the universal energy that makes all this mystery happen. As a psychotherapist and a coach I feel that this is the main event. I can identify a client's problem when I recognise, with their help, which of these relationships is in trouble. You might want to try that for yourself too.

Can closeness in a relationship exist?
Are there more ways than one to be close (e.g. physical, emotional, spiritual)?
Does the closeness move around from one element to another?
Do you require all aspects to connect to feel closeness in a relationship?
How do you create more closeness in an area where you feel it is lacking?
Do you give more love to those aspects that aren't lacking or do you contract?
When looking closer at what is, can your perceptions change and your heart open?
Do you believe that the heart can only grow and expand with love?
Is love the ultimate and what we are looking for? Do we need to love ourselves and others?
Can we give something of ourselves, if we do not have it in ourselves?

Is it a constant quest to find out who we are and to be true to ourselves?

Reflection

This heartfelt Quest raises powerful questions that are worthy of being explored with our partner or personal friends or anybody that matters to us. There is another approach that you can take with these Quests. Write the questions out on a card, one question per card. Turn the cards over. Then each person randomly picks a question to encourage an open-hearted conversation.

Is my happiness dependent on other people around me?
Can you create happiness around you?
How do I make others happy?
Can you create happiness around you, even when others are not happy?
How do I just focus on my own feelings?
Who would you have to be before you could be anything to anybody else?
Is it true that when I am happy others will be happier too?
Can an unhappy person make another unhappy person happy?
Is it possible to stay happy at all times?
Can happiness have many faces?
How do we deal with the negative thoughts?
Is acknowledgement the first thing we seek before understanding?

Can happiness be achieved with will power?
Do you require will power to practice acceptance?
How powerful are the mind and our thoughts?

Reflection

This is the Quest of the power of the mind. Our thoughts are powerful. We believe that we are our thoughts. Is that true? Am I the thoughts I am having? Really? Because I don't remember creating the thought before I gave it to myself. Where do thoughts come from? I am comfortable, even renewed, knowing that I can hear my thoughts and pause and then engage in a conversation with that thought. I don't want to believe every thought that I have. I want to know that the thought rings true for me, that it belongs to me – the real me, not the made-up version of me.

Do I have a soul mate?
Do you have a soul?
Does it linger in space?
What does linger mean?
Is it dangling, waiting to be rescued?
Is a soul in a state of helplessness?
Is helplessness a state of soullessness?
Do you have a soul or are you soulless?

Where is my mate?
Where are you?
Where are you?
Where is anybody?
Is anybody everybody?
Does anybody care?
Do you care to be my soulmate?
Is it possible that all souls are soulmates?
Is a soulmate supposed to be your life partner?
Can you have more than one life partner in a lifetime?
Can you have more than one soul in a body?
How big is a soul?
How big is the universe?

Reflection

What is a soul and where does it reside? It was curious that this person asked whether the soul lingers, whether it dangles. Then I thought of the soul needing to be rescued. Maybe there is some truth in that. What does rescue mean and what does the soul need to be rescued from?

Where do we live?
Who are we?

Can we be us?

Is we limited to us?

Could we be the universe as a whole?

Could the universe live in the tiniest of spaces/places as a whole?

Is this explorable?

If it is, what would the vehicle of transportation look like?

If consciousness could take you there, what would it look like?

How do we become conscious?

How do we be?

Does being require doing?

Do we do?

Do we?

To be or not to be?

Is this a question or a statement?

The question is... is love the answer?

Can the answer become the question?

What is the question?

Is what the question?

Reflection

This Quest becomes one about the universe and consciousness, the idea of 'being'. I liked where we got to 'to be or not to be' – is it a statement or is it a question? If it is a statement then do we choose to be? And if we choose not to be, does that mean that we choose to do instead? To me 'being' means presence and presence is where everything happens without doing. Our natural state of being pulls us towards our purpose and onwards on our path.

What do we know about the universe?
Is the universe within you?
How do we fly to the moon?
Do you know how to grow wings?
What truth is there in my wings?
Can you truly fly on a falsehood?
Is love the guiding way?
Is there more than one way?
Is love within us?
Can we exist without love?
How many stars are there?
Would you be upset if you knew?
In flying, do we fly into the visible or the invisible?
Is the journey inward or outward?
Are the stars inward or outward?
What happens when you close your eyes?
Is there us or we?
Is oneness plural?
So are we the sky?

Reflection

The Quest to know an answer came from the question "How many stars are there?" and makes me wonder about our obsession with knowing the answer. Answer-driven thinking makes me feel there is only one right answer and the pressure of finding that one right answer – like a mathematical equation – is the goal. Life is not about the one right answer. Life is finding what is right for us at any given time. What's right for me may not be right for you. It's more knowing that I am trying to discover what may be right for me that makes me feel good about any decision I make. I also enjoyed the question "Is oneness plural?" I'm on a new thought path with this one. Does oneness embrace plurality? Without the many, can oneness exist?

Do others ever need us?

How would you feel if you were needed, by someone/thing that needs you?

Should I feel anything?

Are you alive if you don't feel?

Are you alive if you don't feel needed?

Do you need yourself?

How does one know the answer?

Reflection

If I had a chance to add another question with this Quest I would have responded at the end with "How does someone know the question?" That's the purpose of Questing in a nutshell.

Why am I me and you, you?
Are we the same?
Where do we come from?
Does that matter?
Our journeys are different and yet our paths have crossed... why?
Is it the mystery of the universe that everything is created on purpose and for us to experience it as magic?
The universe is infinite... is it important to understand this concept?
Is it important to experience it?
Why is it that experiences are experienced differently?

Reflection

I am stumbling onto some curious nuances with Quest. Check this out. Read the last question first and follow it with the first question. Tah-dah!

Is there a God?

If there is one where would he be?

Is God always going to be a he?

What is always?

Why don't we ever learn?

Does ever have a beginning and an end?

How long is a piece of string?

How thick is the string?

Does it need to be thick?

Do we need anything?

Who can say?

Are we back to God?

Have you ever been near that place?

Do you recognise me?

Is this something like a God question?

Am I your reflection?

How can I really know?

Who is asking me?

What?

Are you losing your hearing?

Am I losing my courage?

Reflection

I keep reading this Quest. It is curious, playful and insightful. We were sitting in silence exchanging questions and then I was asked "What?" which of course can be interpreted in many ways. And then it concluded with a big thought provoking question, "Am I losing my courage?" Read this Quest backwards – you will be intrigued.

Will my daughter respond well to my relationship?
Are you responding well to your relationship?
Will I get to where I want life to be?
Are you already there?
I am hoping that I will withstand, will I?
If you needed courage where would you source it?
Will I find the courage and the patience?
How strong is your desire?
Life has unexpected turns, turns for a brighter better future happening?
Is that a choice we make regardless of what turns we experience?
Uplifting is my home beautification program. Will my daughter be responsive to receiving good life changes positively?
Can you love her regardless?
Can trying, being tenacious, responding and yearning bring true fruition?

Reflection

This person couldn't help but provide a response before giving me the question. It shows how challenging it can be to not answer. The questors' questions were seeking answers as if I was a fortune teller. The questions were breathless and they felt that they were being shot out of a gun. I wonder what would have happened if I answered with yes/no?

| **Quest Impressions** |

What others have said about Quest:

» The process is like taking deep steps into the quietness inside yourself. There does not have to be meaning; questions do not need to be answered. There is no purpose or right or wrong; it is just about a quiet mind and whatever emerges.

» Very insightful! This experience has left me with a not-so-comfortable realisation. However I feel I have turned a corner in my own personal growth.

» What question am I thinking of and how has it affected my everyday life? To question with a question starts an inward journey towards what inspires and directs us. Where it ends no one knows, but it will lead back to the start and on to the end and that will be the beginning of finding the truth: the ongoing journey.

» The Quest experience made me ponder the 'big' questions. Initially I felt constrained and my first response was with answers and the difficulty in posing the questions – and the 'right' question. Later on I felt freer 'winging it' and not trying to seek or pre-empt an answer in the questions I asked.

» I found that after the performance I reflected overnight on the questions I had raised.

» This was mentally stimulating and I realised how much the brain can expand its thoughts. It was fun and there were no limits to how far it could take you: from beginning to no end.

» Absolutely hilarious as all questions seemed to lead to sex! How is that? Perhaps I am completely one-dimensional after all.

I found it very difficult a) not to speak and b) to find questions. Finding answers is easy but creating the question was not so easy. Also, directing my thoughts to one problem and not letting them scatter proved quite challenging.

A great experience, making us stop and think about ourselves. The 10 minutes given to this exercise is actually 10 minutes of self-growth. I wish it had lasted longer.

I'm amazed that the first paper offered fitted my question perfectly. It was fascinating, fun and challenging. For me it's all about letting go of fear, having the courage to create and not worrying about other people's judgement such as 'You're being narcissistic!'

Quiet experience and a sense of being humbled and the result was - less pressure to give input/feedback. Many thanks for hearing me and not judging.

What a challenging, but exhilarating experience. At times I felt stuck by my own thoughts but would do it again…yes!

I feel more in control. I can impact my own destiny. Just need to keep asking.

Very thought provoking, gives greater thought process with no dialogue and word comments with questions.

I found the silence very comforting. Made me hear what I didn't seem to want to hear. In some ways it made me realise that maybe if I listened to myself properly I wouldn't feel so confused. A very different experience altogether.

Quest with a friend

You:

Me:

You:

Me:

You:

Me:

You:

Me:

You:

Me:

You:

Me:

You:

Me:

| Quest By Yourself |

We can't always find another person to Quest with, so this approach will allow you to Self-Quest. It's simple and it is inspired by the classical mind-mapping approach developed by Tony Buzan. Write your question in the centre of a page and draw a circle around it. Now write as many questions around the circled question as come to mind. They must be questions. I would encourage you to create at least 21. Twenty questions plus an extra one for good luck! The 21 questions will appear to be random. Allow yourself to let loose and express whatever is on your mind. This is very different to the Quest exchange between two people. The Quest exchange questions are connected with each other's questions, though at times the link may feel tenuous. Self-Questing, like mind mapping, is about getting all the questions onto paper quickly. We want to override the rational mind, which is why you do this exercise as quickly as you can. I want to push you to challenge the depths of your subconsciousness, which is why there should be at least 21 questions. Once you have completed the Self-Quest, it's time to review. Grab a couple of coloured markers. One colour is used to encircle the questions you find intriguing and wish to reflect on or even take action on. The other coloured marker is for the questions that interest you, but you are uncertain whether you wish to pursue. When you have done that, list the questions that have the most appeal, the most intrigue. How different are these questions to the question in the centre? It is this final list of questions that will drive you forward. On the next page is an example of Gabrielle exploring her main question "Will it Work?"

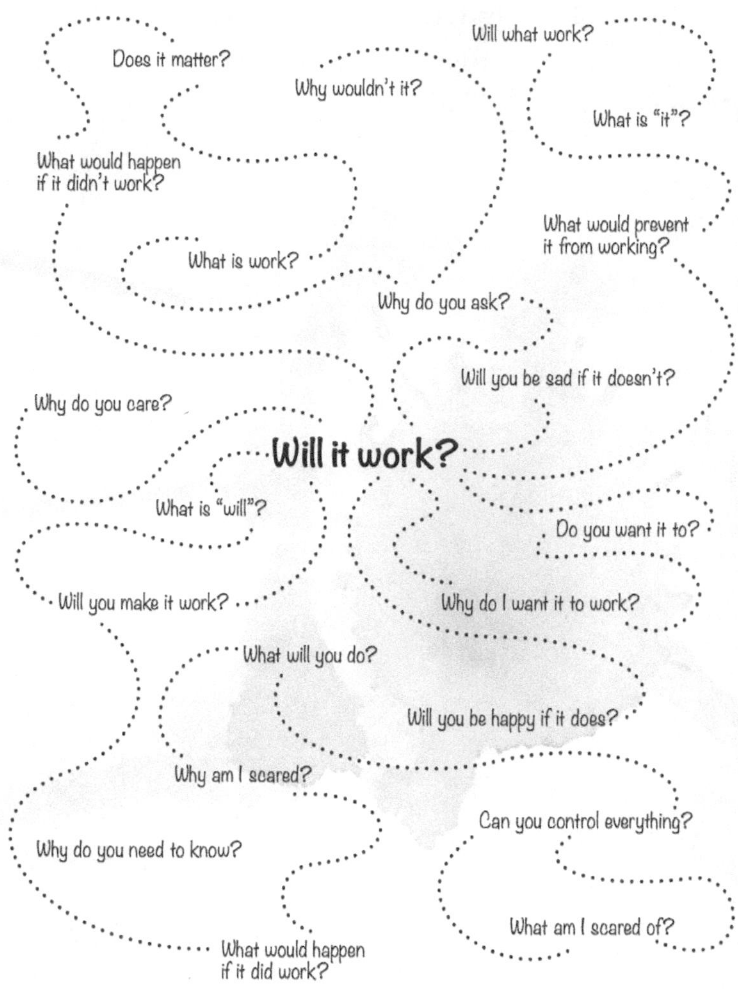
Does it matter?
Why wouldn't it?
Will what work?
What is "it"?
What would happen if it didn't work?
What would prevent it from working?
What is work?
Why do you ask?
Will you be sad if it doesn't?
Why do you care?
Will it work?
What is "will"?
Do you want it to?
Will you make it work?
Why do I want it to work?
What will you do?
Will you be happy if it does?
Why am I scared?
Can you control everything?
Why do you need to know?
What am I scared of?
What would happen if it did work?

Gabrielle then selected these questions to delve into. These are her most appealing questions:

Why do you ask?
What is work?
Will you make it work?
Why do you need to know?
Why wouldn't it?

Gabrielle is a young career woman. She is 22 years old and I asked her to participate in this self-quest. She completed the Self-Quest on her own and in private and then when she came to hand it over to me she said "Wow, now I want to Quest my last most intriguing question with you." I asked her what she got out of the experience of Self-Questing. Her response was a game changer. "I want to do this on a regular basis, even daily. It took no time and I am now reflecting on what really is the matter when I doubt myself. And writing it out is more valuable than sitting there and thinking about it. Something happens when you write it out. You can physically see what's on your mind."

I asked her why she wanted to Quest with me and Gabrielle said that once she could see her real concerns through Self-Questing, questing with someone else would add another perspective. I couldn't have wished for a better experience for Gabrielle.

Interview With The Author About Quest

This is a transcript from a recorded interview. I have removed the questions to allow my voice to speak to you directly.

In the beginning Quest was simply a fun thing to do, just a conversation of questions. And I remember when I first started doing Quest it was just about having some fun. And in having fun, with having that kind of intention, it meant that my responses were somewhat funny, because that was the space I had in mind. "This is fun, I've got a funny response for this one." Very quickly though, as questions began to repeat themselves, I realised that I wasn't honouring the process and I felt that I wasn't honouring the soul of the other person. At the same time I wasn't honouring myself. So then in a very short period of time, I went into a deeper space, and each Quest then took much longer to complete. It was no longer just a quick exercise of exchanging questions. It was about sitting with that question and really connecting with that question. I realised that I was interpreting that question and I was accepting my take on another person's questions. The change in my approach meant that I was inviting something else into the exchange, something personal, intimate and honest.

Questing in silence is important. I wanted to suppress the voice. You know, sometimes talking is hard work. The person listening interrupts many times, wants to guess what you are saying or simply talks over you. At other times I find myself listening to seemingly endless explanations that are not leading anywhere. When you write a question down, you have actually created something, because it now physically exists on the paper. And it is handed over to somebody else to then reflect upon. The person receiving the question needs to make that question their own, as if they are asking the question of themselves. Because the Quest is experienced in silence, there is no opportunity to ask "What does that question mean?" So they have to decide for themselves, they have to make sense of that question themselves, and then once they do, they respond with another question. And so it goes on.

I want to encourage people to ask questions. I want people to feel smart when they ask a question because we are such an answer driven society, it makes me think that the problem comes from people's idea of what 'intelligence' is. And if intelligence means having answers, then the last thing that you want to do is ask a question. It is the same thing with children in the classroom. They often don't ask a question because they believe it will look as though they are not smart. Yet a question is the root of all curiosity. Why does a rainbow have seven colours? Questions like that are what propels scientific enquiry anyway.

The two most common questions I get during Quest

are "How are you today?" or "How are you feeling today?" – something along those lines, and the other one is "What is the meaning of life?" (laughs). The first one suggests to me that they are uncertain about how to begin a Quest, so they ask about me. The next one feels to me like they are thinking 'I only have five questions so I'm going straight to the point'.

I remember one person, this was at Sydney Contemporary Art Fair, he asked me how I was doing, and my question was "Why do you care?" Now you can read that any way you want to, and I know he was offended, and he came back with a response about something to do with "Isn't it polite to ask somebody how they're doing?" (laughs). It was something like that, but by the third question we just got into our Quest.

I learnt after my first endurance art performance, which went for six hours, not to drink a lot of water. (Laughs). So the next endurance, which was I think the longest endurance Quest I've ever done, went for nine hours, and there were no breaks during that performance. So yes, there is some preparation – it is important that I've had a good meal in the morning, that I have nourished myself with water, that I've gone to the bathroom... And then I pretty much just munch on an apple during the performance, whether it goes for six hours or eight hours or nine hours. That's it.

What happens to me mentally in those performances, once I sit on those cushions and enter the performance space... well that's it. I really create my own space and I'm actively working on the space that people are entering. So from that moment onwards, that's it. I meditate internally – so even though I may not seem to be in a meditative state, I am. And this is something people comment on a lot, that there is a sense of stillness when they enter the performance space and sit down with me. There is an intensity to the space.

There are some questions that take me longer to sit with than others. And in that respect, I guess that would be the closest thing I would consider as a challenge. I guess there's one challenge, when people come to Quest, and they experience extreme emotions - sometimes people are laughing a lot or crying. And sometimes they just burst into tears. And that I find very hard… especially because I'm doing an endurance Quest. I don't break my endurance, but I need to ensure that I always have somebody close by who is able to manage that. I mean it's not that I want to go and fix everything or make everything better or anything like that. But I do want to let the other person know that everything that they're experiencing is perfect for them in that moment. And that there is nothing wrong with what they are feeling.

Also, the responses I give them are not the psycho-babble type of responses they seem to expect – it is not about 'why don't you trust the present moment' type questions, it's not like that at all. It is more about whatever I'm called in that moment to reflect upon – that is what I respond with. And I don't even know what this response is going to mean for them. So my responsibility is just to be real in that moment.

I find that Quest creates a dual situation where the teacher is also the student. And the student is also the teacher. There are dual roles without a doubt. There are times where I have sat with people in a Quest and both of us have had tears rolling down our cheeks.

At the end of a Quest performance, I am sitting there in silence after experiencing one question after another question and engaging with so many different people. And then I finally step out of that space at the end of the performance and every-body is gone. There's nobody around. I don't really want to talk necessarily, but I have got all of a sudden, a whole bunch of ideas. Lots of ideas. And a lot of energy, and I want to get into my studio and I want to do something.

The first thing that I do as I finish Quest, before I say anything at all, is to gather all the people who are around me at that time. We gather together in a circle and we 'ohm'. So it's a beautiful primordial sound that we are sharing, and it's a great way for me to bring my voice back to the planet. And to thank everybody who has visited in the last moments, and to be grateful for their participation. There is not much else going on for me, I'm really still in that altered state in a sense. It is not an altered state as in I don't feel like I'm here, I'm very much here, very much grounded, but at the same time, things look really different... people look different, world issues feel different. So I call that an altered state. A drug-free altered state.

Have you ever wondered why is the word quest in question?

Always keep Ithaka in your mind.

Arriving there is what you are destined for.

But do not hurry the journey at all.

The
Creative Journey

Introduction To The Creative Journey

Desire is what fuels our passion. Without it, our passion becomes like a sleeping beauty, lost to the world of dreams. Passion, if you have it, identifies something that we truly wish to pursue. But it is the relentlessness of desire that will awaken our passionate dreams. Desire rouses us to take action and to bring the dream to life. And when the two connect, there is a sense of freedom.

Freedom is when we face our fear, fear of failure, which is our need for the right answer and control of a predetermined outcome. When we can face our fear our course changes, pointing us to our true north. The honest journey begins and little else matters. Not even the destination, nor the rewards, or the feedback. Nothing matters more than the voyage itself, life's voyage, and it's up to you to take it.

If we could remain still and calm inside while we are in transit on the outside… If we could be at peace on the inside while we explore this outrageous world… If we could accept life as it is, rain, hail or shine, and still maintain our focus and not be discouraged, keeping our destination in our sights… If we could be comfortable with who we are yet welcome a better version of ourselves… How differently would we experience our journey through life? Would we become greater creative's?

This section of the book explores two aspects of our lives that are intertwined: our desire to create and our desire to be accepted for our true self. This is the pathway to becoming a greater creative. To create in the face of fear and to be authentic, honest and accepting of who we are. These are our twin voyages. One cannot be experienced without the other. Our creativity requires authenticity, which is self-expression, and our authenticity requires creativity, which is the expression of self. Authenticity in creativity is the search for our voice. Finding our voice is our own way to express ourselves. Like our thumbprint or our signature, no two creative voices are alike. The creativity in our authenticity is how we find out who we are when we are not wearing labels such as father, mother, sister, writer, manager, counsellor, BFF, etc. We need creativity even to understand the question "Who am I?" or "How are you, You?" because we cannot examine ourselves using logic.

What follows is a series of short essays on topics that you may come across along your journey. I offer no answers. Of course after reading Quest that shouldn't surprise you. The essays are more like log entries, journal notes, deliberations, observations and musings made over the many years that these topics have surfaced for myself and those around me. Throughout my own journey, I have experienced an inner peace (and at times excitement) reading someone else's writing about the very same experiences yet written in a different manner. This is what I hope for you, the reader, to feel when you read these journey notes. Perhaps you will find parallels in your own creative journey. When you read about something here that has been similarly challenging for you, that perplexing something that has prevented you from knowing how to navigate, perhaps now you will see it differently. For when you see differently, you will have changed your perspective in such a way that the Laestrygonians, those mythical monsters from the poem representing our fears, will begin to shrink.

I do have an invitation for you at the end of most of the musings. The invitation is called *Make Your Mark*. They are exercises to feed your imagination. Please do not let your rational processes usurp these moments. Instead, allow yourself to play and get into the habit of doing each exercise many times. Give your imagination time to kick in, especially if you have disengaged with it over the years. Many of us do not take the idea of using our imagination seriously. We do not work with our imagination as enthusiastically as we do with our rational thinking processes. Indeed, we undervalue this inherent gift that breathes potential into everything we do, every feeling and every thought we make. Instead, we choose to still the voice of our imagination, though it ruffles and stirs up excitement within us. There is a feeling that the imaginative response is too dubious and until it is tested to death we should not offer half-baked ideas. What of all those De Bono workshops and lateral thinking programs and mind mapping techniques? What of all our motivational speakers engaged on the topic of creativity like Sir Ken Robinson and Elizabeth Gilbert and all the researchers exploring what creativity is like Mihaly Csikszentmihalyi the author of the book called *'Flow'*.

Our tendency is to fall back on rational linear thinking in all aspects of our lives. Not all aspects of our lives are rational, so how have we come to think that rational thinking applies to finding a solution to personal relationship matters for example? There is nothing rational about falling in love. There is nothing rational about love changing. There is nothing rational about why you become passionate about a particular cause or a certain painting or about many of your personal choices. What if we could befriend our imagination and learn how to connect and communicate with this voiceless powerhouse of a resource? How might it change our life? How might you and I change? How would our change impact others?

I invite you to play with the exercises at the end of most of the following musings on creativity. They are designed for you to have fun, a key ingredient in invoking our imagination, to be completed easily and quickly almost anywhere.

I also invite you to participate in the meditations, which follow on from the *You Are. Creative* musings, which are more about personal growth. These musings aim to reveal your authenticity and the meditations will take you into the silent part of your being, the well-being of your being, where the unaffected part of you resides. This unaffected part of you is your true nature, the You of you.

Self-Awareness

The Socratic words 'know thyself' ring true today, just as they did in the days of my Greek ancestors. What did Socrates mean by these words and why are they still relevant? Socrates, if you were here sitting with me pondering your words, I want to know what you meant? How can these two words have created such a failure in my thinking, because I can't find a response that sticks. At once I say of course I know myself and then I waiver and think "Well how do I know that I know myself?" So here is where I have come to berth. The translated Socratic words 'know thyself' can also be translated as 'recognise thyself'. Re-cognise, to be cognisant of self, to see myself again in the same situation and ask the question, "Am I still the same person?" Re-cognise, to see myself in new situations, who am I now? How do you know who you are? Why do others see us differently to the way we see ourselves? I learn something about who I am every day through the things I do and the choices I make, through the way I feel about something and how I react and by noticing and reflecting on what matters to me and what doesn't matter.

As human beings we are perfectly imperfect and each of us is encoded with their own unique perfect imperfections. The imperfect is not the wrong part of us. The imperfect is part of who we are. The imperfect challenges us to see aspects of our nature that ruffle us. Imperfections come as a surprise most of the time and because of this we feel vulnerable. Imperfections awaken our concerns and fears of not being good enough, smart enough, talented enough. Yet this is part of re-cognising all parts of who we are and instead of wishing our imperfections to disappear we could hold onto this part of our self, this imperfect part, and discover what's underneath the fear?

Self-awareness is the ability to observe myself. I observe and I reflect. At times I observe how I judge myself. When I re-cognise this I ask myself this one question. "Who do you think you are?" I pause on the word 'think' because it emphasises one way of knowing which is through thinking. But there are other ways of knowing. Asking this question grounds me and brings me back to allowing myself to witness my vulnerability without judgement. What happens next is a bit strange. I feel stronger. Why stronger? I begin to see the exceptions to the rules I have created around the idea of who I think I am. And each exception to the idea of me brings me closer to who I really am. I feel stronger because I no longer am embarrassed about my beautiful imperfections.

To 'know thyself' is a life long journey and perhaps even the purpose of this human beingness, a personal pilgrimage to our sacred space of self. Could our purpose then be to take action to seek this path to knowing self?

To some extent, this whole book is a process of self-awareness: The interior map helps you discover aspects of yourself, the way you behave or respond in any given situation; Questing helps you see how you think and gently shifts your perspective where needed and the musings that follow are like our conversations stirring you to find your own conclusions and therefore grow self-awareness.

At the end of the day, there is no one wrong, just as there is no one right. But there is a you, a one and only you and though this path of self-knowing may not be easy, it can still be fun and amusing. Maybe we should learn to also develop a sense of humour along with humility.

Soul

When I write of the soul I am not using the word as defined by any religion or metaphysical philosophy. I call on the word soul, as a way of identifying a part of you that you are yet to witness: the better part of you. As our human beingness changes over the years and evolves, always becoming more aware of its self, that self is our true nature and this is what I term soul. To that extent I would like to introduce you to your ultimate soul-mate, the You of you.

The Laestrygonians and the Cyclops,

angry Poseidon – do not fear them,

you will never find these things on your way,

if your thoughts remain lofty, if fine

emotion touches your spirit and your body.

The Laestrygonians and the Cyclops,

the fierce Poseidon – you will never encounter,

unless you carry them inside your soul,

unless your soul sets them up in front of you.

That Is.
Creative

Claiming Your Creativity

You can't claim your creativity if you don't believe creativity belongs to you. So here are three questions to review before we start on this topic:

1. Are you creative?

2. Do you believe you are creative?

3. How do you define creativity?

Take a moment and write down your responses. The answer to the first question is a simple yes or no, but I wonder if your first response was "It depends", to which my response would be "Depends on what?" Does it depend on your belief? Well, that's Question 2. So maybe you compromised and said "Sometimes" to the first question. This then takes you to Question 3.

Sir Ken Robinson, a thought leader in creativity, has said that to realise the true creative potential in our organisations, schools, and communities we need to think differently about ourselves, act differently towards each other and learn to be creative. He not only believes that we have a creative potential, but in order to activate it, Sir Ken identifies the need to learn to be creative. Creativity is learnable.

Creative is not synonymous with artistic ability. We need to extend our understanding and definition of what it means to be creative. It's no use looking in a dictionary. The term creative is hostage to our personal definitions and bound up with our value judgements to boot!

I often ask my students at the beginning of an art program "Are you creative?" They mostly say "No", "Sometimes", "It depends on the situation", or "I can't draw a straight line", "I don't have a creative bone in my body", "I'm not good at art", "I can't reproduce what I see in my head", "I was encouraged to spend my time on practical pursuits", "Whatever I attempt to write is pathetic", or "I need to learn technique first".

Many of these responses are united in the underlying belief that to be creative means you must be able to draw (this is the main reaction) or paint, sculpt or write or express yourself in some magnificent artistic way. When I show students that they can draw and they draw and paint something representational, the response I generally receive is that their efforts are not good enough because they do not have the ability to paint with the eloquence of Michelangelo or Leonardo da Vinci. It seems that the learning process is thrown out the window when adult students come to learn painting, drawing, journaling for writing and every other expressive art form. It seems that there is the idea that you either have it or not – talent that is. It seems as if attending an art class alone will unlock our hidden talent and if it doesn't, then that means we don't have any talent to uncover. We don't have the same expectation when we are learning to play an instrument, or learning a new language or taking cooking or singing lessons. Learning in these instances requires continuous training even when the early results are amateurish and this is understood. But there is something very personal when it comes to the expressive arts because you are not holding an instrument that needs to be learnt, or reading a recipe or learning breathing techniques so we can sing. I think part of it is related to our drawing and painting experiences as children. Everything was good until we were told that trees aren't pink.

Attending an art class or a writing course or any of the expressive art courses, is an opportunity to recover and unfurl your talent.

Every day we make (create) decisions, we make (create) friends, we make (create) love, we decorate (create) houses, we make (create) mistakes, we cook (create) food and we think (create). We are indeed creating and therefore are creative. The question is not "Are you creative?" but "What are you creating?"

Fundamentally, if you believe you are creative you are and if you believe you are not creative, you are not.

Unless you believe that you possess the power to be creative, you will not be motivated to access your creative potential, let alone be able to activate it. That is the power of belief.

Habits of thinking, having the very same thoughts again and

again and again, are what create a deeply rooted belief. One of the most significant findings in psychology in the last 20 years is that individuals can choose the way they think.

No-one can convince you to change your beliefs. That is a journey only you can take and it requires willingness on your part – willingness to be open-minded, to explore other views and to listen with curiosity while suspending judgement. However, before the willingness kicks in you need to be aware that your beliefs are not universal truths and those that are negative are holding you back. This is what is known as limiting beliefs in positive psychology.

Is it possible that you can learn to change your beliefs, you might ask? I think so. This process is called learning. Ask yourself this: do you believe that you are capable of learning? If you answer yes, then you are teachable. You can learn anything if you believe with certainty that you are capable of learning. You can learn to paint, to draw, play a musical instrument and to think creatively. You can learn anything. The question comes back to you. Do you want to learn? I'm returning to the importance of becoming aware of underlying limiting beliefs that may be holding you back and preventing you from fully accessing your creative ability and potential.

Even so, there is one more cord I need to tug.

You are aware of a need for change; you believe with certainty you can learn and are therefore teachable, but do you have a strong enough desire? And there is the tug and the rub all rolled into one!

In order to claim creativity, you must, at least on a rudimentary level, believe you are creative. Once we can say that we are creative and truly believe it, we can put a stake in the ground, fly a flag and claim the territory as ours! Why is this important? We need to belong somewhere on the continuum of personal expression. We are perpetually creating. There is no time that we are not creating something. Take your stake, make your mark, find your voice and understand this once and for all!

When I ask you to claim your creativity, I am not necessarily asking you to call yourself an artist. That would be like asking you to call yourself a chef because you are a great cook. Both an artist and a chef are professions. If you have chosen these professions as a full-time occupation, then go right ahead and call yourself an artist.

Being creative is not a profession. It's an act of doing.

Make Your Mark

Time to reflect on the questions raised at the beginning of this musing: I would like you to create a mind map in response to Question 3, where I ask you to define what creativity is. Please do not use a thesaurus. I want you to explore your own subjective definition of the term.

1. Lets do a mind map. In the centre of a large piece of paper – A3 size for example – write the word CREATIVITY and circle it. Explore this by brain storming all the pursuits; actions and activities that you believe are associated with the word creativity. This is a freeform thinking process. Allow yourself to write down whatever comes into your mind even if you feel it is silly. Delve deeply! I challenge you to write a minimum of 30 responses, even if you need to pause. That's okay, just keep going. Magic happens when you break through the I'm-frustrated-with-this-exercise barrier. Then sit back and look at your mind map.

2. Look at each word you've written around the word CREATIVITY and ask yourself 'Is it true? Do I truly believe these actions, pursuits and expressions are creative?' If you answered yes then circle that word with a coloured marker. Use the same coloured marker for all the words that you truly believe capture expressions of CREATIVITY.

3. Create a vertical list of all the words that represent the ways you believe creativity can be expressed. Next to each word, give an example of a time when you engaged in this form of creativity. You may need to stretch your imagination and force a connection. For example, if you wrote down gardening, don't hesitate to write down the one time you planted a herb garden.

Please do this and you will begin to expand your idea of CREATIVITY.

Are You Ready To Be a Beginner?

When I was in my late 30s, almost 40 in fact, I began my journey into the arts. I wanted to learn about drawing, painting and ceramics. But in those early days I had a sense of urgency and I wanted answers. I wanted to be shown how to paint with oils and how to draw what I saw in front of me, but I didn't know how to go about it. I didn't even know what questions to ask. My approach was more like 'I want to paint like Matisse but I don't want to be Matisse'. I didn't know where to start, what course to take or anything about art materials. In fact art materials felt mysterious to me. Except for the obvious pencils, lead and the coloured kind, I didn't realise how much artist quality materials differ from student quality and what a difference that makes.

When you are starting out on your creative journey, you often don't know where to begin, even after taking a course (or many courses) in painting, drawing, sculpture or writing.

Without the teacher's prompts, exercises, guidance, suggestions and encouragement, the beginner can easily stall. So we end up returning to this question time and time again, "Where do I start and how do I continue learning?"

The thing is that as a beginner when we are keen to create our focus is, generally speaking, always on the end product, on completion, on resolution. I see this in my beginner art classes. There is an urgency to get the canvas out, the colour palette selected, the brushes, etc. After a few preliminary questions and a quick demonstration, the beginners want to begin. They want to give it a go. They want to paint the still life in front of them in one session and to take it home if it is good enough to show the family. They want my role to be advising them almost on a step-by-step basis what to do next, which colour to use, how to use the brush or the palette knife to get the results that they seek. This step-by-step method, like a colouring-by-numbers approach, may give the students a wonderful takeaway but it can also backfire. The process is more fabrication and less creation than it might otherwise be.

When we are starting out on our creative journey, the first thing to recognise is that the creative process engages with all aspects of our being and that there exists a preparatory phase. Part of this preparatory phase is you. Are you ready? Are you ready to make mistakes and to fail? Are you ready to be a student again and take on the necessary study and adopt the patience needed to move into this new phase of your life? It's not enough to give enough time to attend a class or workshop to learn. It's the amount of time carved outside the dedicated classroom that will count, that will make a difference to you and your creative work.

This preparatory phase is also about understanding the material you are working with, not only intellectually but also sensually. What does the paint feel like as you move it across the canvas? How do the words that you have just written down sound like when you read them out loud?

Then there's the exercises. They're like the warm ups we do before the big event. We do this with our body with slow long stretches before we play sport, so why not before art too? These exercises can teach us something and help loosen us up at the same time.

And what about you? How are you presenting at the moment you are about to embark on your creativity? Are you tired? Do you have things on your mind? Your current emotional state affects your creative preparedness.

The preparatory phase cannot be rushed. Not only must it not to be rushed, it should be slowed down. Slow it down so that you can truly engage with what you are creating. This immersion, the preparation or the research and study phase, will allow you to move into the making phase with greater certainty and consideration. It signals a mindful approach to your art-making. So take your time, enjoy the process and allow yourself the time to learn.

Ruth was creating a self-portrait in mosaics, working in marble. She had drawn her face and transferred it onto the board that she was making the mosaic on. Her creative challenge was to use only marble of one colour, a warm white marble that had variations of white within it. How was she going to represent her image in one-colour marble? There is a diversity of ways. There is the size of the cut marble and its shape – square, rectangular, etc. – and then there is the direction that the marble tiles are laid in.

"Where shall I start? Should I just look at the works of other artists and copy them so I can learn?" asked Ruth.

"In a way, yes. But don't copy their work. Seek to understand their motivation, their inspiration, what it was that they were responding to. Understand why those mosaic artists followed a particular rhythm in their line work. Some artists may be portraying an emotion others may be portraying photorealism in their mosaic. When you connect with the work of another artist, seek to find out what it is that resonates with you. In this way you may learn something of yourself and how you wish to portray yourself, " I said.

Many artists have found themselves stuck and unable to work at different times in their career.

One way they learned to deal with this was to change their state. This is an important lesson. How do you do that? By being willing to do silly art exercises and find meaning in them. By being willing to do things backwards and upside-down and finding significance in that.

When you are feeling blocked or stuck creatively, then try

exercises like drawing with your non-dominant hand, which will actually help you to re-gain access to your imagination. What appears to be simply fun and nonsensical can turn into something much more. It may trigger an idea – a composition for a painting or a story. Being frivolous takes away the expectation of creating something important. This letting-go process is when the imagination feels welcome to come and play.

Still think it all sounds a bit wacky? Artists have been using strategies and techniques like these throughout art history as a way to access alternative states of mind and unleash images and ideas from their subconscious. We see this with the Surrealists, the early twentieth century movement of a group of revolutionary artists who believed in the power of the subconscious mind and strove to liberate the imagination from logic, rational thought and the prison of conventional bourgeois values.

When we think of the Surrealists we automatically picture a group of artists and writers chain-smoking and drinking endless cups of coffee in a French café amid heated, passionate debates. Meeting frequently in this manner, the Surrealists played collaborative drawing games, discussed the theories of Surrealism and developed techniques such as automatic drawing and a funny little game called 'exquisite corpse'.

Exquisite Corpse, 'cadavre exquis' in French, is an artistic or literary process by which a random collection of words or images is assembled by each player adding to the composition, having only had a brief glimpse of what the previous person contributed. This was generally achieved by taking a sheet of paper, drawing on the top third of the page, then folding it over so that most of the image was concealed and passing it on to the next person. Without any real idea of what was already there they would add to the page before folding the paper again, hiding their own contribution and passing it on to whoever was sitting next to them.

The Surrealists aimed to create paintings and writings which would revolutionise all aspects of the modern-day human experience from the personal to the cultural, social and political. They wanted to free people from what they viewed as the false rationality and restrictive customs and structures on which society was built.

Free your mind, release your need for certainty and outcomes and allow yourself the opportunity of finding your own voice.

◁ Make Your Mark ▷

Let's draw like the Surrealists. No pressure here to make anything look good – however you define good. Grab six A4 sheets of photocopy paper. Hold the paper in portrait format and then fold the paper horizontally in thirds. You are going to create a family of figures. And of course you will be drawing with your non-dominant hand. This drawing is usually completed with three different people drawing the three different parts of the body. If you don't have another person or two to complete these drawings, it's okay. The following steps are designed for you to complete this exercise by yourself.

1. Keep the paper folded. Using the top folded third of the page, draw a head and neck. Any head, any neck. Proportions don't matter. Be playful. Be cartoon-like if you want.

2. Draw heads on the remaining five sheets of paper.

3. Fold over the heads so you can't see them. Mix up the papers. Select one of these papers. You are now going to work in the middle of the paper. Draw a torso – a body with arms but no legs.

4. Draw torsos on the remaining five sheets of paper.

5. Fold over the paper so you don't see either the head or the torso. Do this on the remaining five sheets of paper. Mix them up again. Select one. Now draw the legs. They can be wearing shoes or not, they may be dancing or standing straight.

Once you have finished, unfold the papers and see what you have drawn. Enjoy your family of figures. Give them names if you like.

Variation: Cut the pages up in their thirds and continue to mix and match heads with torsos and legs. You can also have fun using animal heads, bodies or legs mixed in with human shapes.

You might be wondering what the point of this is. The point is to have fun, to let go of what we think is a good drawing and allow ourselves to pursue an activity for the sheer joy that it brings. In the early stages of our art journey it is key that we allow ourselves these kinds of creative adventures. You might wish to revisit some of Picasso's drawings after this!

Talent

You have decided to become an artist and you are a late bloomer. Or you are an art enthusiast and wish to devote yourself to this avocation. You attend art courses or even art school and you practise. You read books and study Old and Modern Masters. You watch videos about artists' lives, read blogs, surf the Internet and continue to practise.

Yet the journey you have undertaken doesn't go as smoothly as it should. Why can't you create the way you want to immediately? You are an adult, so you should be able to learn new skills and execute them quickly, right? You have the desire; you have the determination, yet you are not seeing results.

Disappointment turns into anxiety and in no time those uninvited thoughts kick in. You begin to question your decision to pursue an artistic journey. Then that one negative thought sparks a rush of unhappiness that leaves you with an even deeper feeling of uncertainty, which has now spread throughout your body so the work you produce becomes contracted and hesitant and even rigid. You begin to doubt your ability to ever produce an original result that would make you proud. And then of course there is that serious concern about having any talent anyway. Without that, what's the point?

Art techniques are teachable. Technique is not to be confused with having or not having talent. Art techniques are like learning the alphabet before you can read and write. So if art techniques are teachable, the question then is, are you teachable? You might think you are because you attend class or you study by yourself, you do exercises and you are motivated. However is there something that may be stopping you from being 100 per cent teachable – those limiting thoughts that live uninvited and rent-free in your headspace. How did they get there anyway? Pause a moment. Close your eyes. Listen to the voice in your head. What's it saying? That you are wasting time? That you should be doing something useful? That what you are doing is self-indulgent? That you have no real talent? That you don't have what it takes to express yourself creatively?

I have raised this question before in another musing in this book, but I feel it is appropriate to ask it again. Do you believe that you are capable of learning? Yes, of course you do. I can't imagine you saying no. Whether you *want* to learn is another matter. The point is, if you believe that you are capable of learning then the only uncertain thing is how long it will take you to learn. Would it bother you if you took longer to learn a technique than someone else? Does taking a long time to acquire a technique mean you have less talent? Perhaps it just means it takes you a long time to acquire a technique!

You are an adult who has decided to pursue an artistic or

creative life. Perhaps you feel pressed for time because of your age or because you have a job or career that takes up a lot of your time. That's fine. Don't let these thoughts distract you whilst you are learning, whilst you are a student. If you do, you are not making the most of your allotted time. If you concentrate on your lack of time, then you end up focusing on short range strategies, like following step-by-step instructions on how to take perfect photos every time or on how to create a masterpiece in oils or the top one thousand words to use to become a bestseller. Refocus. You have given yourself permission to study in the field of the creative arts and to be a student. Don't forget you are starting from scratch with all the advantages of your wisdom and experience!

Approach your studies, whether on your own or in class, with enthusiasm and joy and do not demean the value of the lesson because you feel it hasn't helped you become what you think you want to be. Take and master each and every lesson. Determine the personal value each lesson holds for you.

Let education ignite the fire that fuels your creativity.

Talent means hard work. I'm not talking about the hard work required to develop your talent, I'm talking about the hard work to recognise the talent you already have. We are all individuals. You know that. You have heard it all before but I'm asking you to stop, listen and then 'get it'. There is no other person on this planet right now who is exactly like you.

A cat in a hat once said "Today you are you, that is truer than true. There is no-one alive who is you-er than YOU." Remember this and thank you Dr Suess!

Do not fail to recognise your own special spark. Trust your talent. It is there. You were born with it and it is your responsibility to discover, nurture and use it. Do not deny what you, and only you, were given to create with. Each time you create something go 'WOO-HOO!' or say 'Not bad' and smile even if it's crap, because you are one step closer to revealing your own artistic language. Always say thank you and be grateful for the experience.

Now, here is what you have been expecting to hear: practise, practise and practise. Put in those 10,000 hours and become the expert. How many stories do you need to hear before you truly accept that this is a journey? Okay, here is one more:

'Les Demoiselles d'Avignon' took Picasso nine months to complete with a documented record of 809 preliminary drawings. Surprised? You shouldn't be, because he was tenacious. He was prolific. He made art his life.

And nothing has changed today. People who succeed (insert your definition of success) persist tenaciously, attentive to their passions, their yearning, love – whatever motivates them and drives them on.

Practice is another word for training. We expect this from athletes and musicians. They work hard for many hours a day. If you want to be a professional artist the demands on your time are no different to working a 9-5 career day. This shouldn't stop you from pursuing your talent, but it should discourage you from comparing your results with those of an athlete. Having said all of that, I have seen amazing works of art from people who have consistently dedicated their spare time to their practice. Set time aside. Be realistic with your time too. Your art will appreciate that dedication.

For all those late bloomers who are venturing into the arts, remember that every problem and every challenge you have faced and resolved in your life has been a process of creativity. This is a testament to you and your creations to date (home, career, relationships). I want you to remember this as you venture into the arts and consider that this is just a new kind of learning, a creative learning that will require discipline. It will ask you to be dedicated to learning, to be disciplined to your craft and to be consistently motivated to practise.

Whenever you feel discouraged, just think this: next year will come with or without having made any art. Choose which direction you will take - the one that allows you to grow your art practice and self expression or the one that says "I didn't have time." We all have the same amount of time. How we use it is a choice. There are times that our priorities will change, like taking care of loved ones in need. This is where we put our brushes and pens down for a while. A while. Not forever.

We cannot help but *create* in our lives. It is very hard not to create and so to some extent whether you respond to what's tempting you or to social, family and work obligations, know that you will still be leading a creative life.

Everything we do is an act of creation. Creativity is simply the way we express ourselves – the self. The way we dress, speak, our home environment, garden, how we cook, the words we choose to communicate, the relationships we attract and therefore the way we connect with the world – you and I, we have created it all.

So maybe it's not lack of talent that is stopping you from learning to make art. Maybe it's your lack of inclination, will or desire to express yourself through the arts.

You are a creative being – it's impossible not to be.

Make Your Mark

Open your journal and draw a border close to the outer edges of the page. Hold the felt tip pen or pencil in your non-dominant hand. When you are ready, make your first mark, any kind of mark. Allow whatever movement your body or mind chooses. This is a short, sweet, gestural mark. Avoid the impulse to go ballistic on the page. Once you have made your first mark take a deep breath and then look at it.

Stand back and explore your connection with the mark without judgement. Imagine the mark is symbolic and meaningful and that it is inviting you to make another mark. What should the next mark be? Don't use your rational mind – work with your intuition. Your intuition will feel like a pulse, an inner sensation. If you are having difficulty connecting, simply pause for a moment. Close your eyes. Using your imagination, transfer your attention to your feet. Feel the tingling in your feet and slowly bring your awareness up to the lower part of your body called the hara. Gently open your eyes and continue to look at your journal. You will sense the movement your arm wants to make. Release the movement and make another mark.

This exercise alone, repeated many times, will change your belief in what a drawing is and where it comes from. After you have done this several times you may want to research the Abstract Expressionists. You can watch artists painting in this manner on YouTube. The only difference is that you will see them using brushes and paints instead of a pencil.

Process, Practice, Progress

I want to know who I am and the process of making art is like a pilgrimage that always takes me there, to those places that show me who I truly am, those places that reveal myself to me.

This may not be the same experience that you have when you make art, but it happens to me, because before I set sail on my art journey, whether it's a commissioned work or my own, I set the celestial compass to my Ithaka. That is, I clarify my intentions from the start. This may sound something like 'I intend to approach my art with endurance, patience and trust, to take no short cuts and to accept that at some point I may think my work is ugly and I will probably question my ability to produce a work that vibrates with honesty. Because I know this, as I go I will learn. So I will follow this process and trust my ability to discern as I go.'

To some extent I could say that I set myself up with art challenges that will stretch me. I am not always certain that I know how to execute a particular exhibition piece or commission. There is fear as well as deep joy when I face these uncertainties. I get to see something new about myself that I didn't know before. These new things are insights and they are not always positive. They are not always pretty. This non-pretty stuff is what is called in psychological terms 'shadow work'. It is the dark and hidden side of our psyche. However it's only shadow work if you do the work. That means you need to look at those parts of yourself and not hide behind excuses and justifications. This newfound self-awareness is often enough to transform us into a better version of ourselves. But… (yes, there is a but) often we spend too much time explaining and justifying the negative traits that we found when we descended into our own darkness. On one level that's fair enough, but (yes, another but!) fair enough keeps us anchored to the same place where it is more than likely we will experience the same thing again and react in the very same way. Self-awareness is taking responsibility for the way we react. It is no-one else's fault and to some extent it's not your fault either. Taking responsibility is empowering because you can change you, you can't change another. Accepting this allows us to begin the journey to deeper self-awareness and once you do this, shifts happen.

I work in a variety of mediums (oils, mosaics, clay, bronze, encaustics, words) and they all have one thing in common. They have been around for many years. Old methods and techniques appeal to me. They cannot be rushed; in fact they require patience and endurance. Each medium brings out something different in me. When I am writing, words become stories and as I write I wonder what is it that I am really wanting to say. My intellect is on a mission as I search for a way to express my experiences and intuitive process in words. Painting challenges me the most because of my underlying limiting belief that I am not good with colour. Of course the more I believe that the more it becomes true. When I work in clay or encaustics, the material and I become one. My experience when working with these two materials is rhythmic and natural. It feels like we belong together. And my encaustics are colourful – go figure! When I am creating I am searching, I am exploring, I am continually solving and resolving. I have to work with and accept the uncertainty of not knowing how things may turn out. The gift in this search for meaning is clarity.

As a therapist I follow the unknown, often hidden, messages and underlying discomfort of my clients and when it is safe, when it is right, I bring them into full view – to be seen and to be witnessed. This is like playing a game of hide-and-seek. Once we have found whoever was hiding the game is over. No one can hide there again.

I facilitate creativity in others. If needed I counsel the inner critic like Ganesh, gently removing those invisible, of varying sizes, shield-like obstacles that stop creative juices flowing.

Now we come to my September story:

In September I enrolled in an online art course which seemed simple and fun – a sort of doodling and mixed media painting course where you worked on small pages using limited resources: pastels, water colours, pens, pencils, inks and acrylics. I had all of these things. So I signed up.

Every lesson was guided and beautifully expressed and

explained with a video and a demonstration. All students on the course were encouraged to share their work in a private online forum.

But the other students' work was amazing! How could I put my naïve attempts at the exercises up for comparison? I couldn't. And I didn't until… until I recalled my purpose in enrolling.

My purpose was to remember how it was to be a student and this is what I learned:

At the start of every new project we are enamored with the idea of the big picture, the final outcome. We have a vision we want to see come to fruition. Sometimes we want the fruit before the tree can bear it. I leant to take the time to develop the best environment needed for the tree to bear fruit. I know that as I am writing this book, I need to accept or reject my editor's comments that appear in a bubble at the side of my manuscript. How easy would it be for me to just press 'accept all changes' from the tracking menu bar? Then my book would be finished and ready for printing. Yet this process of writing, rewriting, deleting paragraphs, editing ideas, sorting through my message is what the tree needs to bear fruit. It's the process of nurturing your art patiently, painstakingly and with love.

I have learned that every time we start our work, we begin where we are at. 'At' is this precise moment and where we are 'at', at any given moment, encapsulates all that we have been and not been.

I have learned that when we all meet up at one location, an

art course for example, we each bring with us our own 'at'. This is where I am at, attending my new art course.

So now I feel the strength of vulnerability. I expect nothing more of myself than to be a student, to allow myself to be guided and not let my artistic reputation get in the way of becoming a better artist. That only comes when I can accept where I am 'at' and dare to allow myself to falter, to fluctuate, to teeter and to hesitate while I find my growing artistic voice.

Our beginnings are filled with uncertainty, exploration and a search for meaning. If I can remember this at each new beginning – and any one journey may contain several new beginnings – I will no longer wish to hurry my arrival. Instead I will experience the gifts inherent in the simple act of making the journey.

Let me say this another way: I am conscious of my creative process and how I bob up and down in the creative waters giving birth to an idea. I know that sometimes I sit on the shoreline looking and wondering what's out there, too uncertain to make a move, but I have learnt that sometimes not moving helps me to connect with my work at a microscopic level – to see something previously unseen. I know now that I have benefited from this because the 'aha!' moment has been sparked.

Art is a process and you have a personal creative process to unfold.

Art is a practice. Never stop your training.

When you know how you process and when you dedicate

time to practise, you and your work will progress.

Once I hit rock bottom with a commissioned mosaic cross. I was gluing down each piece of cut glass, each dedicated cut, one triangle, square, oblong, at a time, but the glue was changing the nature of the design I had created. I took off the pieces, cleaned each piece with a toothbrush and water and then cleaned and resealed the surface of the cross to start again. I did start again, only to have the very same experience. So once again I removed the tiles, cleaned them with water and a toothbrush and, washed down the surface. Again. And again. I was giving everything I had to this small commission and I was left barren. I was personally connected to the work. The commission had come to me from two sisters whose mum had passed away. They came with a wish to have a mosaic cross inserted into a heart-shaped blue pearl granite headstone. It was a privilege, I felt, to be given such a commission. Then, two weeks after I received the commission, my mum passed away. One night I left my studio feeling depleted. This piece of work was just not coming together. I took a different approach, hoping that the barrier would reward me with an unexpected insight. And so it came to pass. I meditated and asked why I felt inadequate and then I wrote in my journal and this is what came through:

You have stopped seeing. You are disconnected from whatever wishes to be expressed in your work. You are holding onto what YOU want said through this commission. I want you to see what you are pushing away. I want you to see what you are not letting go of. You are to do the work, not be the work. Let go of how you think it should look. Let it be what it wants to be. Follow each cut. Place each shape down with care, love and honesty. Let the work surface from your heart's hands. Accept each piece that is placed. Accept me, the unknown, the uninvited.

I have learned to appreciate a message from the uninvited – this feeling of inadequacy. I have learned to appreciate the strength and courage required to look inadequacy in the face and try to understand. This commission was for their mother, not mine. I understood that. I realised that I must be mindful and consider the purpose and intention of each piece of art I embark on. I do not need to know how it will look, but I do need to set my intention, my destination, my Ithaka…

Let the work guide you. It's not for you to control, to say it must look like this or that. Allow the material to speak. Give your hand permission to move the way it likes and to express itself in the way it wishes. I had been commissioned to do the work. I was asked. The sisters were not making the work. I was. And I did so on their behalf.

Make Your Mark

Grab a 2B pencil and paper. The paper can be photocopy paper or, if you have time, buy a very small art journal that you can keep in your pocket or bag. Personally, I like to draw on brown paper rather than white.

If you like you can make a very quick, handy journal with two sheets of A4 paper or by cutting up brown paper bags. The size I like to work in for this kind of exercise is 10.5cm x 14.5cm in landscape format. You create this size by folding a sheet of A4 paper in half long ways. Tear the paper along the fold so you have a rough side. Then fold this long strip in half again. You now have two sheets of folded paper and eight surfaces to draw on. If you slip one paper into the other you have a booklet.

This booklet can be used for all the drawing and writing exercises in this book. The first thing I do is draw an outer border by hand – never by ruler. That is what I call capturing the space. And that's what happens when we draw anything – we are capturing a shape, creating an enclosure with our pencil and our line.

All drawings are to be completed with your non-dominant hand. What I would like you to do is create eight consecutive drawings with your non-dominant hand of anything that may be present and near you. They could be of a glass, another pencil, a book or your smart phone. It's not about what you are drawing. It's not even about how good your drawing looks. It's about beginning a journey of non-dominant-hand drawings and finding value in repeating shapes.

St. Repetitus

Distractions in the form of random thoughts are constant interruptions. If the brain is being interrupted continually then our ability to think clearly or focus deeply on the task at hand, whether an art project, a conversation or a business decision, is limited and impacted.

How can we give our fullest attention to the present moment and live our present experience? How can we stop these random thoughts from changing our priorities so as to continue to pay attention to whatever we are doing?

When we stay fully engaged in what we are doing, we give novelty the chance to emerge. Novelty cannot be hurried. It does not come to the frenzied mind. Novelty comes when we are focused and paying attention to what we are doing. Novelty savours repetition.

Often in classes I ask my students to repeat an art process over and over again with the same subject matter, usually a pear. They respond with long sighs. The idea of repeating the same thing over and over again bores them.

This is the story I share with them: I call it Morandi – St. Repetitus. Giorgio Morandi, whom I have written about in *Introduction - Practising Starts*, began his art career painting in the style of his contemporaries. Then he began painting bottles – ordinary bottles and jugs and the occasional ramekin. The same palette prevailed throughout his paintings, the same tints of colour and subtleness. The works were quite small. Slight variations appeared through his use of a horizon line, a horizontal line that broke up the background in two places. Apart from teaching art, he created these images of bottles again and again. Hence I have dubbed him St. Repetitus.

I ask my students what might have sustained his interest in painting if all he ever did was the very same subject matter in a limited palette on small canvases. Too hard a question I know, so I ask them to copy one of his works, any one of his works. I ask them to study any one of St. Repetitus' paintings of bottles – such an easy theme – and reproduce it as best they can. Only after many failed attempts do they realise what was missing from their own skill set and then they happily paint more pears, knowing that something magical will happen for them as it did for Morandi and those who appreciate and delight in his work.

Our skills are anything that we have repeatedly and mindfully practised. A skill is something we have practised until it has become hardwired into our brain and can be repeated effortlessly. What has been discovered by the scientific community and written about in medical articles, in newspapers and in motivational books is called myelin. This is how a repeated action affects the circulatory connections in the brain. These new connections become like superhighways when the mindfully practised action becomes automatic through a process called myelination. New skill superhighways can be created at any age (the brain is plastic; it is not rigid: it continues to grow throughout our life) and at all times if we practice mindfully.

Myelin is proof that practice makes perfect. Long live St. Repetitus!

Make Your Mark

You may have seen this exercise coming! Please repeat the eight continuous drawings from the previous exercise that followed *Process, Practice, Progress* but this time do not allow the pencil to leave the page. You will need to cross over the surface of the shape you are capturing on the page and when you do your drawing will take on another energy. No erasers please!

Mistakes

"In my studio I practise… hence the name… studio practice."

Imagine approaching your art-making as research. Maybe you already do. And if you don't, how might that be different to the way you currently approach it? Let's say you want to try out a new medium. Perhaps it's working in inks, encaustics, clay or printing.

What do you do? Join a class? Google? Ask a colleague? Find a book on the topic or perhaps go to the art supply store and ask the retailers or maybe just buy the materials and give it a go?

If you approached your art making as research, which is to search and search again, would any part of your searching be considered a mistake? I imagine not. And if you say yes then, okay, call it what you want… just keep doing it! Because you are discovering along the way.

When I create I am process-focused. That means I follow a 'way' not a technique. My process involves meditations, writing in my journal, doodling, reflecting and being open to the world channel - messages from the universe. I include an intuition-based research approach in my art practice and I usually have Joseph Campbell close at hand saying, "Where you stumble, there lies your treasure." I do hear voices!

My 'mistakes' viewed by others, counter my growth. My 'mistakes' viewed by me, are research. And the more research I do the more I learn.

So it is okay to keep making mistakes because it means I am prepared to sit down with the results of my own uncertainty and to have faith in my own creative process. My mistakes guide me. They correct the course of the path I am taking. Good on you, mistakes.

Make Your Mark

Grab your drawing journal and sketch a border around a double page. Pause for a moment focusing on your breath. Soften your eyes as you look at the page you have just drawn the border on.

1. Sense what you are feeling. Name it. When you have made the connection between yourself and a word, pick up your pencil with your non-dominant hand and allow your hand to respond to this word with a doodle. This doodle may be complex or simple. There are no rules. Trust that you will know this doodle represents the word you connected with.

2. Check in with yourself. What do you sense now? Is it the same or different? Either way, repeat Step 1 and create another doodle that represents the new sensation. You may wish to do this several times.

3. When you have completed this, go back to the first

drawings and look at them upside down and sideways. Each doodle has four perspectives. What do you see each time you turn the image around? This is one way of forging a connection with your work, by looking at it in different ways and seeing something that was not obvious before.

Once a student of mine called John was agitated when he arrived in class. John was responsible for 80 staff members in an IT company. His management style created a lot of stress because he had a tendency to take the fall for many of his staff's errors. He had a 'buck stops here' attitude. He was empathic towards his staff because they worked exceptionally long hours.

I asked John to take a few breaths and feel what he was feeling. Then I asked him to go into his body and sense what he was sensing, then to name that sensation as best he could and draw it out. He continued until he completed the exercise and was reflecting on Step 3 when he had his 'light bulb' moment. John's drawings were around the word bully. He felt he was being bullied by his boss and he didn't want his staff to experience that. When he began to turn his images around he saw a number of silly images. They were so ridiculous that he began to laugh. How could doodling the emotionally charged word bully create such silliness? That was his revelation. He saw what he needed to do back in the office with his staff and himself and his superior. I'm not suggesting that you will experience anything like John did through this drawing exercise, however it does highlight how shifting perspectives in life and in art can be interrelated.

Results Are Here To Guide Us

When we are creating we are making. And making means we are building something. When we build we gather our materials and put them together creatively. This applies equally to cooking, writing and painting, to name just a few 'doing' processes. So if putting materials together is building, then taking them apart must be unbuilding. Unmaking? And that's okay, right? Or is it? How do we feel when we are unmaking? Generally when we undo something it's because we believe we have made a mistake. Errors need to be erased or corrected. Either way, we end up describing this process as something that is not positive.

Taking something away, subtracting, removing, reducing, obliterating or even abbreviating may feel as though we are starting all over again and starting all over again feels as if we have wasted time, that we have made a mistake. And making mistakes, well, you know how we have been taught to respond to a mistake. We make (actually we create) a mistake and then we associate with the mistake. We somehow transform that error, glitch or boo-boo into a personal trait. We are now flawed. We are not creative enough and therefore not talented. We have just become under-confident.

Yet intuitively we know that art is a process and a practice. Art allows us to explore. Each time we create we do so from the beginning again. I paint lots of pears. I feel like the Morandi of pear painting at times. I know it might seem I am obsessed with Morandi, yet each time I sit down to draw or paint the same pear in the same light and setting with the same pencils or palette, the pear never ever looks the same. I can draw or paint a pear without a real pear in front of me as well and even if I do that, I never draw the same pear twice.

The repetition of making art doesn't mean replication. Replication is not mastery when it comes to self-expression. I fall instantly in love with some of the pears that I create; others take me on a journey of falling in love. That's the role of results. Each time I make something I get a result that guides me towards an action which may be to add or subtract, to leave or remove, to reduce or start again – not because I made a mistake but because I am being guided along the path of making.

Snakes And Ladders

You know how sometimes you fight with yourself about your art? When you say that you are not good enough or that your talent is limited and finite, that you are talented only up to here, this point, this imaginary line, when you hit the heights of your creative abilities and feel mediocre?

This is precisely when you should dare yourself – dare yourself to be ordinary and dare yourself to do your mediocre best, because in there, in the finite bounded by an imaginary line, there is a ladder. This ladder will take you to the heights of your ordinariness, where you will realise your uncommon, individual self-expression.

Usually when we are creating or producing something we fear our work is not good enough, but when we do we overlook what is staring right at us, daring us to pick up the clue and work it out. This clue, this breadcrumb, is the one small thing that is unusual, that will become your mark, your special signature and no one else's, your distinct voice if you can only recognise its potential and the possibility.

How do we get to extraordinary if we haven't landed on ordinary first?

This is the value of finding your ordinariness and turning

it into the extraordinary. I apply this approach in my own art. I look at my work and seek what it is I do that seems to be nothing particularly special. When I spot it I magnify it and when I do that, something extraordinary occurs pretty much (well almost) every time.

When I was creating a mixed media mosaic depicting the branch of a peppercorn tree, I had to work the background design in glass tiles, which I don't like working with. The branch was made out of uncut and unpolished opals and other curious and beautiful mixed media. The manufactured glass tiles were ordinary and looked commercial in contrast to the beautiful organic opal rocks. I began to cut away each of the four perfectly straight machine-manufactured edges of the 2cm-square glass tiles. I wasn't particular about my cutting, so sometimes there was a 10-degree angle and at other times I ended up with a rounded edge. I walked away knowing, or rather trusting, that when I returned I would see the extraordinariness in the material. And I did. What happened was that the organic and accidental shapes I had created produced a beautiful painterly effect when I laid them next to each other. I now have a new approach I savour when working with glass tiles.

Of course this may not occur each time, but if you don't look for the extraordinary in the ordinary it will never occur.

I dare you now to seek out the ordinary in your work.

Why Do We Have An Imagination?

I'm asking this question because often when we engage our imagination in problem-solving or coming up with ideas or experimenting with our art, we are told to 'get real' – responses like, "that's not how it should be done" or "you're wasting your time" or "it's been tried before" and sometimes just long silences of dismay.

Real is contrasted to imaginative in a negative way. It makes me feel that imagination is fake and not to be trusted. If so, then why do human beings have the ability to imagine? Is it not to make things come true? Do we not conjure up and invent and work with our imagination and ask 'What if?' first, before we research it, test it and see if we can make it real?

We define a person with natural talent as someone who has been endowed at birth with the ability to pick up any pencil, paintbrush, lump of clay, camera – pretty much anything – and create something of equal value to Michelangelo or Rembrandt or Ansel Adams. For a more comprehensive list of names, please Google artists who have made the most highly valued art works!

What if we step back for a moment and think: we are all born with an innate natural talent that is ours to explore throughout life. Imagine that! But wait… that's a clue, isn't it? To imagine it. Imagination is a gift we all have, is it not? How often do we use our imagination during the day? Or are we caught up with what's happening to us: a job we don't like but which we need in order to pay the bills, a relationship that is losing its lustre, the feeling there is no time to do what we really want to do – what was that again? Scuba diving? Well this is it, imagination, the elixir of the gods!

Imagination is the gateway to our creativity. Why then are we not using this shiniest of thinking gifts from morning to night?

"By believing passionately in something that does not yet exist, we create it. The nonexistent is whatever we have not sufficiently desired." Nikos Kazantzakis

I pick up the thread of this beautiful quote calling on us to reflect on our belief (putting aside passion for a moment) in our ability to create. Beliefs are often hidden, asleep in our subconscious, waking only when we are about to take that first step towards expressing ourselves, that step towards being creative. Limiting negative beliefs about our creative potential do more harm than good. Do not confuse negative beliefs with critical thinking – they are more like niggling, bad-tempered criticism. Unwelcome them!

Nikos also spoke about passion being the quality in us that drives our ability to create. So, is it possible that those 'can't do' and 'am not' thoughts that we happily, readily, unquestioningly repeat kill our passion to create?

How our beliefs got here in the first place matters less to me than knowing that they exist, for this is the first insight. Explore your thoughts. Ask yourself when you hear one of your thoughts about your creative process: "Is what I'm thinking true?", "Do I truly believe that of myself?", "Why do we have an imagination if we do not question our own status quo?"

The Inner Critic

Art can mesmerise us, provoke us or make us feel safe, it can antagonise us or create a paradox, all with the sweep of a paint brush, the click of a camera, the sound of a pen running across paper, even the sound of clay oozing into form.

Its creation fascinates both the maker and the observer. We want to know the artist's thoughts and methods, while they want to know the viewer's reaction.

Why do we make art and what role does it play in our lives? I have been exploring these questions for many years and can see a curious trend that stretches from art in the early ages to the art of today. The bones of some of today's art look like the scratching of cave drawings or sophisticated children's works, all very beautiful and perhaps even divine. I feel that there has been a return to soul, a move away from realistic reproduction and towards an inventiveness that calls for the imagination to wake up and share its vision, its experience of all the sights this outer world has to offer. David Hockney explores his outer world in this way, especially in the portraits he created with a series of Polaroid images. He takes many images of the sitter from different angles: low points, high points, from the left and from the right. He then recreates the portrait of the sitter by assembling several images taken from different angles. The result is magical. They are captivating and absorbing and reveal more about the sitter than a single photographic representation.

The artist's journey must make inner sense of outer objects. It takes courage to be objective and to dare to explore the intimate and esoteric.

These are my thoughts as I begin to record my own creative process. I have done this many times over the last two decades, but have only just realised how much it can change. The changes are subtle, but I feel a key turning, a door opening a little wider, a nudge beyond the boundaries set by my previous works.

My hand, my eye and my mind all collaborate to create. My hand follows the rhythm of my heart and my eyes follow my interior vision while my mind critiques the hell out of them both. I'm laughing as I write this. It's one thing to know that this is what happens, but quite another to see it written down challenging me, daring me to find my way through it. I'm smiling because I know each of these elements plays a vital role in my art.

I honour my hand pursuing the calling of my heart, my heart being the voice of my body's knowing. My normally muted heart comes alive and guides my hand as it crawls and sprawls across the page at the beginning of an exploration – for all drawing is an odyssey.

I am exploring space: nothingness and emptiness, the darkness from where everyone and everything comes, awaiting the light.

When the light arrives it slices through this darkness and lands… somewhere – it must land somewhere. The light finally coalesces into a form, one I haven't seen before. That's when the mind kicks in and tries to appreciate the work, but usually ends up making some silly comment instead, something like 'It looks like a goat. Are you making a goat?' I ignore it and continue to work.

My eye, my inner vision, is activated and awakens my imagination, encouraging my hand to keep exploring. I'm considering the naked surface of the canvas now as I have moved into colour. Everything changes again as light breaks through the darkness and splits into an infinite array of colours. I am getting excited.

This is dangerous ground for me because usually this is where my mind steps in and says 'Okay, you've got it. I'll take over and finish this for you now. I can fix this.' It's the point where my mind interferes and wants to make sure the work is pretty, that it is acceptable to outside observers and to my own internal critic. Forgetting that I am following my soul, the mind introduces a new audience.

And so I write a letter to my mind:

My dear spirited mind,

You work so hard to make me happy. I recognise and appreciate that.

I hear you in the background asking questions like 'What are you making?' and wondering whether it is good enough. Your curiosity makes me question my ability to make art, causing me to retreat into 'research', to buy another book or do another online course or watch another 'how to' video. I just want to say thanks, and as a sign of my appreciation I would like to offer you a promotion.

My dear spirited mind, I would like to appoint you as Chief Creative Appreciator of all my creative efforts, sculpting and painting, drawing and teaching, writing and speaking or simply being. If you feel you do not have the right skills for this position, I am willing to offer you a lifelong training program to help you realise your potential.

I am offering you this position because I feel that we both want the same thing, but are approaching it from opposite ends of the spectrum.

I am coming from a place of exploration, discovery, love, acceptance and reflection and you are, well, basically you are scared that I might be judged foolish. Which may in fact be the case.

I just want you, my dear spirited mind, to know that I can handle the opinion of others. Good or otherwise. I am okay. Really. I won't collapse in a heap, I won't freeze and say I will never make art again. There is only one voice with the power to do that to me. And that voice belongs to you.

How about meeting for coffee to talk about how we can live and work together more productively?

Yours, Noula

It is indeed a daring act to create. To work with your soul, to gather your inner resources and to appreciate (not depreciate) your creative efforts so that you give birth to what you are destined to bring forth. We are incomparable human beings, able to create: to create art, to create life, to create relationships, to create communities… Each creation is an act of daring.

We are not alone though and we have the gifts necessary to achieve our goals. We all have imagination, the art of the mind, and intuition, the art of the soul. This is my assemblage – bringing them all together, hand, eye and mind.

Mutter, mutter, blah, blah, blah…. these are the uninvited sounds of the inner critic that talks to us – always unkindly – lacking compassion and a comprehension of the power of positive thinking. What is that all about?

The inner critic is the author of toxic thoughts: 'No, don't do that, you aren't good at doing that, you are not talented, that person doesn't like you, ask someone else to do it because they are better at it, you cannot learn creativity, just go back to your day job.' Perhaps the nicest of all inner critics might say 'don't attempt the drawing until you have all the instructions and make sure you follow them in sequence. That's important because if your drawing is not good it won't be your fault.'

This little voice or that sensation (sometimes the inner critic creates physical discomfort, sweaty palms or nausea) is to protect you from failure. What is the best way to avoid failure? Simple.

Avoid experience altogether, but as we all intuitively know, to evade experience means to shun life.

Experience, from the Latin 'experientia', is knowledge gained by repeated trials. No trials, no experience, no knowledge.

Get to know your inner critic. The inner critic truly wants the best for you. Help your inner critic by listening and reinterpreting and replacing fear-based language with positive language.

Yes, that's right – commune with your inner critic – ideally in writing. Get a pen and paper and write down what the inner critic is saying. Then respond on the same piece of paper and continue the process (almost like Questing!). Let the exchange be one that seeks to understand. Do not fight each other. Accept each other's right to a different point of view – even if the language of the inner critic is harsh. The inner critic has had to attract your attention quickly – that's the strategy – hence the strong, judgmental language.

Each time you do this you will create a wonderfully supportive inner voice and it won't take long before your inner critic becomes your inner coach.

Make Your Mark

One of my favourite exercises that I enjoy sharing in my art classes and meditation programs is journal-writing from the heart. Have a question seeking guidance ready, something about self-doubt perhaps. Write the question down, but make sure it does not start with the word why. Ask "How might I..." The word might, prompts the imagination to come and explore. Might answers are not limited to right answers only.

1. Close your eyes and meditate for a few moments by focusing on your breath, on inhaling and exhaling. Allow yourself to settle into your seat or on the floor, allow any tension to fall into the arms of Mother Earth. Concentrate on your heart space and begin to breathe there.

2. Place both hands over your heart, one hand on the other. Try to feel your heart beat.

3. Using your imagination, drop your 'How might I ...' question into your heart space and then continue to breathe through the nose into your heart space for a few minutes.

4. Open your eyes gently and look at your question. Pick up the pencil with your non-dominant hand and write whatever is waiting to come through. Please don't question the writing or the language. Simply allow the words to be written. Allow your body to experience the sensation of what is being written too. What guidance did you receive?

The Benefit Of Comparing

There are no benefits in comparing ourselves and our works of art to the greatness of those whom we aspire to be. Indeed we do not exactly want to be them. Why would we ever wish to paint like anyone else? All that would come of it would be people recognising the similarity – that your painting is Matisse-like and your photography is David Hockney-like. Then you will feel unoriginal and an imitator (of course a good one) and unimaginative. When you compare yourself to another artist and wish to be like them, you end up being compared to them.

Paradoxically, the one benefit to be had from comparing our work to that of an artist we wish to emulate is that we discover what it is about that artist that attracts us. The truth is that we seek the same talent that allowed them to create the art we admire. Think about this for a moment. The Matisses, the Hockneys, the Elizabeth Gilberts, the Heston Blumenthals, all these greats in the various fields of creativity built and followed their own model of personal expression. We can all learn techniques from the greats, but the most important lesson is how to have the courage to find your voice. That's what they did. Where did they find the conviction to carry on with their personal expression instead of pursuing excellence in a conventional mainstream?

Discover your own magic by reading biographies and stories about your favourite artists and creators. Find out what their challenges were and how they overcame them. Learn about what made them curious, what questions persisted throughout their careers and what they were seeking to resolve. Painters don't just want to represent a pretty bowl of fruit. They are engaged in problem solving. Whether their challenge is harmony of colour like Matisse, the perspective of perspective like Hockney, overcoming personal challenges like Gilbert or recreating feasts like Blumenthal, creators are always problem-solvers.

◄ Make Your Mark ►

This is a reflective writing exercise. Pick an artist whose work you enjoy looking at or reading. Write their name in the centre of your page and circle the name. Write down all the things that you associate with that artist or author. If it's the way they make you feel, try to describe your feelings. Perhaps their work engages you intellectually… When you have completed this, write out all the qualities and attributes you believe they possess. Maybe you think that they were born gifted or that they work hard. When you have done that, research articles about them and seek written and audio interviews they have given. What did you discover?

It is important that you record your opinion of the artist before you explore anyone else's point of view.

Your Interior Teacher

If you are not learning by experience then you are learning through the experiences of others. You have cut short your own trial and error process of learning, by working out how another artist resolved the challenges of composition, colour, form, narrative, line, size, material, etc. Why is copying another artist a good idea?

When I began my transition from corporate suits and tax deals to art books and smocks, I realised that I would have to become my own teacher. The best book I ever bought was Betty Edwards' *'Drawing on the Right side of the Brain'*, where I learned that the eye could be trained to see an unknown, foreign, visual vocabulary that had been, until then, invisible. Before Betty I would draw from Old Master images because I had read that their apprentices learned by copying their master's drawings. So I did the same thing.

I could not copy very well though and I couldn't understand why. Why didn't my copy of Leonardo's sketchbook image of a woman's face look identical – or even close enough? I would have been happy with close enough!

So thank you, dear Betty. I worked through your book and was then free to explore on my own. My interior teacher was able to find ways and methods to improve my work. It took another decade for me to find my voice, but I had grasped the difference between learning techniques and discovering what I wanted to achieve.

Your own interior teacher is resourceful too, in locating appropriate books like Betty's or teachers, mentors, workshops, videos, the lessons you need – your artistic technique, talent and voice can all be learnt. Art is a learnable undertaking.

That's why we have art schools. You may think that art schools are for people who have talent. There is no more truth in that than saying that kindergarten is only for people who have the talent to read and write. We go to school to learn to read, to write, to count. We are teachable creatures and what holds us back is our attitude and how open to learning we are. Are you capable of learning? If you say yes then you are. The only thing that may be holding you back is how strong your desire is. Do you really want to learn how to… (fill in the gap here)? Desire is the key that drives determination. The talent will follow.

What kind of teacher do you intend to become? What are you learning from your interior teacher?

When we create a work of art, whether it is a painting or a sculpture or anything else, the process is transformative. We are transforming the material in our hand into something that originated as a pulse from our body, driven by our desire and our imagination, and we are producing something that was originally invisible.

Will your interior teacher, encourage, coach and nurture you? Or will your interior teacher tell you how badly you're doing, that you have no talent and are wasting everybody's time, that you should find another hobby or form of creative expression? Will your interior teacher appreciate or disparage you?

Find the right interior teacher. I'm sure you have a few to choose from. Fire the ones you no longer want!

Make Your Mark

In your journal I want you to draw a bottle with a 2B pencil. The bottle can be any shape and any size. Once more I am asking you to draw the bottle with your non-dominant hand. Draw the bottle on the longest part of a double-sided page. Turn the journal upside down so that your bottle is now upside down. Use your fingers to smudge the outline of the bottle. Inside the bottle I want you to draw a face. Add eyes, nose and a mouth to the bottle and if it isn't a long bottle then add a neck. If you like you can add a body as well. This, dear reader, is your interior teacher. A kind of genie in a bottle! Is this image kind or is it critical? Whichever it is, I would like you to have an imaginative exchange with this genie of yours. Write out what the genie is saying, or appears to be saying, to you. Write out the genie's monologue next to the drawing. How silly is this getting? You are either having fun right now because your genie is kind and light-hearted and wants to see you and everything you do flourish and grow or your genie is a monster – and now you may just want to toss the drawing out. Please don't. This is a playful awareness process that allows you to identify what your inner self is saying and to recognise whether you are being encouraged or not. Then you can choose what to believe, what holds the truth and what influences your decisions and your ability to learn something new.

Copycatting

There was a time when I would measure my art against that of my favourite artists, living and dead. I didn't realize that my feelings for their work were more idolisation and that the more I loved their work the less I loved my own. I was truly unaware that my lack of confidence in my own work was correlated to my admiration of other people's until I experienced my own Big Bang. This Big Bang is not just a theory – it happened to me. The moment I realised that I felt my own art was unworthy of being seen by the contemporary artists I admired was the very same moment when I began to delight in my own work. I collapsed the imaginary hierarchy of artistic excellence that I had somehow created in my unconscious and allowed myself to pursue my own true path, unaffected by anyone else's beautiful and amazing work.

Without a doubt we can still learn from others, but we should be conscious of what we choose to learn. What I admire in another artist is authenticity. I seek to understand their convictions and what personal qualities led them to create. I mentioned Matisse, Hockney, Elizabeth Gilbert and Heston Blumenthal in an earlier musing, *The Benefit of Comparing*. I wrote that these Greats created and followed their own models of personal expression and wondered how they had the conviction to do that instead of pursuing excellence within the established conventions. That is what you should seek. Think of the inventiveness of Leonardo da Vinci, the energy of Giacometti's sculptures and the way Picasso re-interpreted African masks, creating a new way to see. These qualities of inventiveness, energy and seeing differently are what we must explore in ourselves.

Focus your attention on discovering what your own magic is. You can do this by reading biographies and stories about your favourite artists. Learn what their challenges were and how they overcame them, about what made them curious and which questions persisted throughout their careers. What creative challenges were they seeking to resolve? Creators don't learn a skill like painting so that they can paint a pretty bowl of fruit. They are engaged in a process of problem-solving. Have I said this before? Yes I think I copycatted myself from the *Benefit of Comparing*!

I wish you a Big Bang moment too!

Make Your Mark

This little exercise will take a bit more time, but it is so much fun to do. You will need your glue stick and an image from a magazine or newspaper. Tear out a picture of a person or an animal. Don't use scissors – just use your fingers. The image should be small enough to paste in your art journal with enough room around it to draw. When you have done this, choose a limb or a facial feature or a piece of clothing or, if it's an animal, the mane or tail, and extend the line. Yes, with your non-dominant hand! What you are creating is your own version of what this image will be like when you have drawn over and extended it. Who did this first? Picasso did. He would grab images from newspapers and doodle over the faces, distort some of the features and extend the image by drawing an imaginary background. From these doodles he discovered new images that inspired future paintings. Who knows, he may have been inspired by Leonardo himself and his exaggerated images of the grotesque. Another topic you may wish to research…

Don't Be Afraid To Love Your Work

Whether we are learning to make art or whether we are seasoned artists, our art exposes us and what others may consider to be our imperfections. Particularly as beginners, we tend to see most of our results as rudimentary and imperfect. When we are left to our own devices our inner critic seems to take on an unassigned role of judging our work, mostly nitpicking and highlighting imperfections, leaving us feeling incapable of producing good art.

To avoid this, we cunningly enrol in a course that teaches us the step-by-step process, guided all the way by instructions and the teacher who cheers us to the finish line with our beautiful art work.

Personally I prefer to rely neither on my interior critic nor my external cheerleaders.

What if we welcome our imperfect outcomes and recognise that these works represent the infancy of something that has the potential to be marvellous? If we appeal to our potential will we see something different in either our work or even perhaps in ourselves?

Don't be afraid to love your work at every stage of your creative development!

It's when you tear up the canvas or screw up the paper with disdain that you will find yourself repeating the same frightened, paralyzed attempts. Our bodies absorb our repetitive and self-deprecating thoughts so that when our hand moves to draw something it does so coyly. When we try to write, we just stare at the paper or the computer screen because, well, what do we have to say anyway?

Don't be afraid to care about your work at every stage of your creative development. Allow yourself to delight in it. Pick up the pencil again with enthusiasm and encourage yourself to try again and again, looking forward to watching your work develop.

Your work does not need to be good, fantastic, fabulous or outstanding before you can love it. There is no prerequisite for loving your creations, none whatsoever.

Creative Doesn't Have An Antonym

I wanted to write about how to be a greater creative by exploring the antonyms of creative. I figured that if I could see what the opposite of creative was then I could unlearn it.

The first set of antonyms I discovered were a series of words beginning with 'un'.

Uncreative, Ungifted, Untalented, Uninspired, Unimaginative, Unproductive, Unoriginal.

We can't be an 'un'. Can we be the 'un' of something? Don't we have to be that something first and then not be it? So I started to think that if you believe that you are uncreative then you have certain uncreative qualities.

I began talking to people who believed in uncreativity and I made this list of the words they used to describe their talent at being uncreative. I also asked them to not use an 'un' word.

Stale, Fruitless, Dull, Logical, Imitative.

Discovering what you think about yourself in this 'un' way can guide you away from the unwanted, especially if you don't feel these things really belong to you. For example, you may associate stale with uncreative and yet realise that you are not stale, but just not giving yourself time to freshen up, so to speak.

This is a subjective process and I encourage you to explore yourself and see what emerges. At the end of the day the word creative does not have a direct antonym. It is the absence of creativity in your life that creates the feeling of uncreative.

◁ Make Your Mark ▷

What makes you a gifted uncreative? Answer this question without the use of words beginning 'un' in just the same way as I have written about it above. Feel free to be playful and please do not stop after the first few words. Write a minimum of 21 words – after all, you are the gifted uncreative. Please write this list vertically. Next to it write the antonyms of these words. Now you have two columns. One is the gifted uncreative list and the other you can call the gifted creative list.

Once you have completed both lists, sit quietly, with your feet flat on the floor and your eyes closed. Focus on your breath. Reflect on your gifted uncreative words and sense the feelings that may be surging in any part of your body. Breathe into that part of the body and simply sit with it. After a few more moments open your eyes and write down which list describes you better, the gifted uncreative words or gifted creative words.

Finding Your Tribe

Our tribe is composed of people who make us feel loved for ourselves, who understand what we are going through, accept our gifts and soothe us when we go adrift. Find your tribe. You will never feel lost again when there are people who are your safe harbour or anchors in life. We are not designed to make it on our own. We are at our best collaborating. That is more than sharing skills and desires. The exchange of ideas creates ladders and bridges to new heights and vistas that neither of you knew existed before. Find your tribe where every member can accentuate something different in you.

Make Your Mark

Remember those bottle-turned-into-face drawings from *Your Interior Teacher?* Draw your imaginary tribe in the same way, using your non-dominant hand. Decide how big your tribe should be and draw them all on one page. You might buy some watercolour pencils and add a splash of colour here and there. Just buy a few colours you like and scribble here and there on the page. Dip your finger into some water and smudge the colour or wet part of the page and colour in the wet area. Have fun. Explore. Experiment.

Once you have drawn and coloured your tribe, reflect, if you haven't already, on whom you have represented. Maybe you haven't realised that you do already have a tribe? You may also notice who is missing. Have a look!

And if you find her poor, Ithaka hasn't deceived you.

Wise as you will have become, with such experience,

you will have understood by then what these Ithakas mean.

You Are.
Creative

Honouring Yourself And Authenticity

The arrow in play always lands somewhere!

In class one day a discussion began on mistakes with questions like "What is a mistake?", "Can every one tell when a mistake is made?", "Does a mistake have a universal identity?" In the midst of laughter and metaphoric exploration of what a mistake is, the question "What does a mistake feel like?" emerged.

The amusement was interrupted with an abrupt statement. "Well, a mistake is something wrong. A mistake is not right. A mistake is when you aimed for one thing and failed to get it. A mistake is failure."

To shape art, we begin with an idea. As the idea emerges, if we do not like what is surfacing the criticism starts. In portraiture this is very obvious. The nose is not in the right place; the mouth is too small, the skin colour is not right. How curious. Art is the one place where we should be able to let our imagination roam free, yet we constrain it. And in restricting it, we hold back and even abandon it.

But what if a mistake just misses the mark, like in target practice. The arrow in play always lands somewhere. It can't land nowhere. It is somewhere and it creates a flag for us. Here I am. I landed here. If you want me to land somewhere else, then throw again. If I want to paint differently, can't I change my brush? But then I ask "Why would I want to change?"

"I tried to produce work which was my own, work which was sincere, naive, in accordance with my abilities and my vision." Emile Bernard in *'A conversation with Cezanne'* by Michael Doran.

Cezanne! I love that. "…in accordance with my abilities and my vision." There is something golden in these words. Something was liberated in me when I read those words. It is so very right to honour our abilities.

If we honour our abilities and vision when we work we are saying that we are doing our best – and if we do that every moment of every day our best will grow and mature. When we crush our abilities, when we smash them, we dishonour and disallow that which is naturally ours. Our authenticity.

Make Your Mark

You may think I am asking a lot with this next exercise. So far you have drawn faces from bottles, but now I want you to draw your own face, using your non-dominant hand again. Take a picture of yourself with the camera on your smart phone that includes your neck and shoulders and draw your face from that image. I am not asking you to create a self-portrait, I am asking you to draw your face, so this will be an 'inspired by my face' drawing of your face. Our visual skills are challenged by drawing our own image, mostly due to self-consciousness. We are not comfortable looking at ourselves for long and we don't know how to observe ourselves, let alone anyone else, without the stifling inner critic talking us down. Settle into this drawing with an easy meditation that only takes a few minutes – or even a longer one.

After you have taken a photo of yourself, edit it by changing it into a tonal image. This is a grey scale image, taking away distracting colour. Draw a border on your page so it is ready for you. Are you prepared to meditate? In a sitting position, feet uncrossed, arms and hands uncrossed and your back elegantly propped upright not leaning on the back of the chair, close your eyes after reading these instructions and breathe in and out through your nose. Count the length of every exhalation. Sometimes it lasts to the count of four, other times to the count of seven. At some point your exhalation finds its rhythm and the number remains the same. When this happens continue to meditate, for another few minutes. Once you have completed this meditation, open your eyes and maintain a soft gaze. Begin drawing with your non-dominant hand, using the phone's tonal image of you. I am only asking you to draw outlines. Come back to this exercise and do it as many times as you can. That request comes from St. Repetitus!

E-Vents

Throughout my years as a teacher of creativity and a coach/ therapist, I have observed that many of the questions raised were not actually seeking answers, but were spoken more as statements of fact – representing a need and a wish to be heard by someone compassionate who understood the unfortunate circumstances and the individual's condition.

For example, when someone in art class says "Why can't I draw?" the subtext may be 'I can't draw and that's a fact and you can't change my mind about it, but I would like you to be kind to me.'

I believe it is good practice for our questions to be conscious of any subtext that may be going on. This is what makes Questing powerful. If you skipped that section of this book then you may decide to go back and try it out.

Asking questions when we do not really want to change anything, just to be emotionally soothed, is something we do to ourselves from time to time and it is a very vulnerable state to be in. We are seeking kindness or tenderness or sympathy and this is fine. I have no doubts about the healing power of being emotionally heard and held occasionally. However if this becomes a habit, a coping pattern, then question yourself and realise that the benefits are only short term. Knowing that this may be the motivation behind your self-doubting questions should help you. How? Firstly, acknowledge you are not seeking any guidance or answers, simply the opportunity to rant and rave. Admit to yourself that what you are seeking is an audience to an E-vent – Emotional vent! If you can be honest with yourself then you won't need people to save you. Quite often an E-vent is cathartic – you've got something off your chest and now you can move on. Knowing that you are just having an E-vent means that you don't have to camouflage it as a real question or rational thought. You can have your E-vent and move on.

Let me give you permission to host as many E-vents as you want until you have exhausted them all and can start to express the questions that will emancipate you.

Make Your Mark

To host an E-vent you need someone to play with or you can substitute a soft toy. Soft toys are very good listeners. If you think a soft toy is lame, remember what you buy people of any age in hospital. You may say balloons, but it's the soft toys that patients love.

Sit your listener, real or otherwise, opposite you and start ranting. Soon you will start laughing because this is so silly. A word of warning – E-vents are not designed for serious emotional matters. They are your normal everyday raging against what is upsetting you, consuming your mind and preventing you from moving forward. E-vents are reactions. Expect whoever is listening to you to laugh – and you will too.

Are You On NICE?

Nice is one of those words we use a lot but what does it mean? All I can come up with is that nice means so many things that it has become ambiguous and therefore unreliable. When someone says nice it's meaning is questionable and could be sarcasm or 'niceness'. When I asked my students what nice means, most of them came back with the same response "It means…nice?"

It's such a strange word because we can all see niceness and feel niceness and taste niceness and hear niceness and even think niceness: niceness is what our senses experience as nice. That's nice!

We use the word nice so often that it comes out of our mouth unconsciously, before we have time to think more deeply, rushing the conversation to a conclusion – well that's how it feels to me when someone uses the nice word.

"How was dinner?"
Nice
The end.
"How was last night's outing?"
Nice
The end.
"How was Peru?"
Nice
The end.

We seem to have become lazy and stuck. Why do we use this nice word so often? Are we suffering from niceness? Is niceness an overlaying universal measurement of kindness and goodness that leaves us feeling that we have been nice to each other? But what does that mean?

Another thought develops. Is it possible that the desire to be nice and to experience niceness prevents us from discovering how we feel at a deeper level? Is our ability to develop impaired because of this 'niceness' syndrome?

Niceness is a variety of behaviours, actions, deeds and words that are displayed so we are liked. We may suffer from niceness without awareness, believing that we are just being – yes, you know what I am about to say – believing we are just being nice. Well, isn't it nice to be nice?

I guess it is, but what does that mean, nice? And why do we often have conditional niceness statements like "Yeah it was nice, but…"

My suggestion is to 'know thyself' and be aware of why we do what we do, of what might be driving our words and actions. My quest is a pathway to authenticity. How can you know who you are if you do not know yourself or even know how to know yourself? It actually takes more time and effort to act the person we want others to see, than to discover our authentic self.

⫷ Make Your Mark ⫸

Here is the antidote to the niceness syndrome and a way to discover who you are, a way to become authentic. Remove the word nice from your lexicon. Look for other words to replace it. Carry them with you and use them when you can.

This may slow down your communication as you begin to search for the appropriate word that best expresses what you are feeling. Goodbye niceness, hello authenticity, or at least the practice of authenticity.

Here is a list that may assist you to get started:

Munificent

Mystical

Irksome

Zestful

Saturated

Juicy

Festive

Spirited

Engaging

Encouraging

Soulful

Reflective

You can be metaphorical and use words from the visual or culinary arts to express yourself like the colour blue or the flavour of a spice or you can go wild and compare yourself to an artist, an animal or a wise muse. This way of communicating is playful and engages the imagination. It will take you down some curious twists, unfurl insights and increase understanding.

These are a few simple methods along the lines of meditation and mindfulness that teach you to know yourself. They produce a pause in your automatic responses. In that pause you can ask yourself 'What do I feel about this?' and then be quirky or meaningful with your new words now you have stopped being nice for the sake of niceness.

What Happens When You Don't

What happens when you cannot even take the first step on your journey, when you won't even try because of the uncertainty of the outcome, fear of making the wrong decision and concern over what others may say?

What happens when we don't create, when we don't make, when we excuse ourselves from the creative process because we believe that we are not creative, talented or have anything to offer and that everyone else is better than we are?

Do you not think that this act of absence is in itself creating something anyway?

The absence of making a decision is still a decision. The decision not to decide is still a decision. Does refusing to participate in life not in itself create something that we may not want? Maybe for a little while it feels safer to abstain from actively participating.

It is the same as when we hide our creative efforts to avoid being judged talentless.

This is my response to that concept, to the idea that by not doing something even remotely creative you will be kept safe...

to not go for that job interview, to not speak your thoughts out loud to your partner or friends, to bite your tongue, to hold back and not attempt anything new, to shut down as a better alternative to feeling vulnerable and scared. You stop the sun from shining down on you and stay hidden, but then one day you wonder what this adventure we call life is all about and begin to search for meaning and purpose and wonder if perhaps you have missed the boat. It's never too late – that's the good news. It's never too late to take the plunge, to get wet, to sit out in the sun, to start using your voice and expressing your views even if they are half-baked. To try something new like painting or singing or how to improve your vocabulary – any form and I might add every form – is an act of creativity.

Our souls yearn to make something. When we come to a halt by avoiding or absenting ourselves from life it is our soul and our heart that shut down. Our minds take control to keep us going. Our minds set goals to give us a sense of purpose, meaning and achievement, but once the to-do list is completed there is a vacuum. Addictive behaviour can fill that void and so can blaming others for everything that is wrong… Caught up in this we forget who we are – camouflaged deeply in our to-do lists, commitments, careers and reputations and conversations about what's wrong with the world.

Who are we? Creative beings, without a doubt. Each and every one of us has an individual voice, an outstanding message and a distinctive way of being. This is a journey to learn who we are. We discover who we are through making things, making things happen, generating relationships, communities, families and art – music, books, paintings, even dancing.

In contrast, what happens when you do?

We love to make. We like to feel that we have been part of something. Making can be an abstract concept like a career or it can be an artwork. If it's about making a career (as an accountant, lawyer, teacher, counsellor), then the paths are visible to us. They can be seen. If the way is through the arts and the process becomes inward, we learn to see the map in the dark and make discoveries that only we can make. This is the hero's journey, the unmapped territory that, once entered, allows you to see who you are, where your life will find meaning, where the sun reflects on the gifts you brought with you. Once you have made this discovery you will feel responsible for bringing out this knowledge and sharing it. If you don't, you are creating a life by default.

Hurry Up And Slow Down

Multitasking is a process used to get through a series of undertakings quickly. The focus is on speed. It requires talent to discern what is relevant or important in a particular time frame. That means decisions are made that may compromise the outcome of any of the tasks that are competing for the same time frame. This corporate sought-after trait can occasionally seep into our personal life when we try to compress everything into a given time frame. We hurriedly drop the kids off at school, dash for a takeaway coffee, we call family and friends on a speaker phone whilst driving to the next appointment, we constantly talk about the lack of 'me' time, we squeeze in a movie with a loved one and call it a date – and the whole affair looks like a to-do list that we tick off with a sense of accomplishment. But there is no personal achievement, for although everything was carried out and ticked off our golden to-do list, what was actually created?

Multitasking is a valuable technique in an emergency, but when we extend this to our creative life we are allowing something else to take charge. The 'musts', 'shoulds' and urgency gain control. This sense of urgency prevails when we interrupt a conversation to answer our mobile or to read an email. Our life is run by a time-piece. This time driven approach makes us anxious to fit in as much as we can within the tick-tocks causing us to forever remain in 'doing' mode.

Can we make time for ourselves? Can we make the time to grow emotionally as well as mentally and spiritually? We are more than a body and a mind. We forget sometimes that we have emotional and spiritual paths to travel to and each needs time to grow with us.

When it comes to self-growth and to self-care, patience is needed rather than an urgent approach to complete things, to make things happen, to want problems resolved immediately. If anything is needed urgently today, it is to hurry up and learn to slow down. Slowing down doesn't mean that you are lazy or wasting time. It means that you will not make compromises in personal matters because there is a sense of hurry to get to a conclusion and to move on. Remember Ithaka and allow the journey to take its course.

"Be patient with yourself. Self-growth is tender; it's holy ground. There's no greater investment." Stephen Covey

Make Your Mark

Do you have a meditation practice? Do you want to have one? One of the most valuable tools to personal growth and self care is a meditation practice. You cannot force this upon yourself. Don't make it one of the 'musts' and 'shoulds' of you life. Instead, get to know yourself a little better and understand why you are not meditating. If you are meditating and are happy with your practice you can skip this exercise.

I have a meditation for you to experience. These are all mindfulness meditations because they require a soft alertness, an engagement with the mind. In each of the meditations I would ask you to put aside five minutes. Sit in a comfortable chair with your feet flat on the floor. Sit with your spine straight but not stiff or army like. If you can, do not let your back rest on the back of the chair. The crown of your head should be aligned to the heavens, not tilted back. This means that the chin is parallel with your shoulders. And if this is all way too much, just sit in a chair and try out the following meditations.

Close your eyes. Inhale through the nose and exhale through the nose. If this is hard, then try inhaling through the nose and exhaling through the mouth. This meditation is relatively simple. As you start, notice your thoughts. Just notice them. Let them come and let them go. Letting them go may be a challenge in the beginning because some of your thoughts may call you to action something. Remember that these are only five-minute meditations – it can wait. Each time you have a thought simply go back to placing your attention to the breath entering your nostrils and moving down the back of your mouth and throat. Follow the breath. How far is it going? Is it going into your belly?

After a few minutes of connecting with your breath in this

manner, I want you to count the duration of your exhale. Do this in your imagination. It's the duration of the exhale not the inhale that I want you to count. Some may experience four counts and others may experience more. It doesn't matter. Just focus on the duration of your exhale. As you do, you may find that a thought interrupts this process. Simply start again.

I would like you to keep a meditation journal for 21 days, noting down your experience. Try to make your five-minute daily meditation at the same time of the day – morning is preferable. Feel free to increase the length of your meditation by small increments of one or two minutes as you grow your confidence and your desire to meditate. It's paramount that you know why you want to meditate.

What's Wrong?

One of our most desired and ambitious objectives is to be right. This craving to find the right path, the right partner, the right way to do something, the right way to be, creates anxiety and unfulfilled aspirations. It paralyzes our ability to search beyond safe limits and makes us too scared to place our individuality before our sameness.

Here is the funny thing about wrong decisions. No one ever makes one intentionally.

I could end this topic with that last statement, however I shall continue. We always take the best decisions we can. The best decision is neither right nor wrong, it's simply the best we can make given our emotional state, our financial state, our level of self-awareness and our choices, the best we can do, considering the personal terrain we are crossing at the time.

So how can a decision be wrong? It can't be wrong at the time, but upon reflection and having experienced its consequences, we may look back and say that that was wrong. To me the only wrong is to call it wrong and apportion blame.

Blame and excuses begin when we have difficulty in accepting that we are not perfect – the ultimate word for right! What if instead of going down that well-worn and tortured path we decide to ask "Did I do my best?", "Was that the best drawing I could do at the time?", "The best advice I could give?", "The best care I could give?", "The best writing that I could produce?", "Was that my best intention?"

If you can accept that each and every time you do something, say something, make something, it is your best, then your best will just get better and better. So much emphasis is placed on being right instead of being best. But that's the attitude to take, because doing your best sustains you.

Mistakes, errors and avoiding being wrong keep you in the shadow called fear. It's time to come out and shine by becoming aware that you are doing your best at all times.

Unless of course you're not, in which case maybe it's time you did do your best.

You Can't Get There From Here

You can't get 'there' when you are focused on what's happening here – it's too complicated!

Wherever we wish to go, wherever we wish to be, whatever it is that we want for ourselves, we must move away from 'what's happening here' and move towards 'there I am'. This means that when we are thinking "I can't pay these bills", "I don't like my job", "Everything is taking too long", "My partner doesn't support me", "I made the wrong decision"– situations that cannot be changed – we must move away from what we don't want that has already happened towards what we do want which is waiting to happen.

It is normal to feel unhappy about decisions that have turned out badly or when what we want is taking a long time to achieve. This challenges our faith and makes us question whether we are on the right path or should change course.

This kind of thinking about what's happening here and now is circular. The here and now is what the past has brought us. We go round and around, revisiting what's already happened, looping back over the very same steps expecting to see something different. I hope you are wondering if that isn't the definition of insanity!

Focus on the there and now instead of the here and now.

Perhaps recycling 'what's happened?' may change your perspective and make you see it all differently. Is the difference positive or negative? Either way, you are not moving towards what you want because you are stuck where you are.

Finding possible solutions for the challenges we experience requires a change in focus. Instead of addressing the here and now we might move to the there and now. Mr. Eckhart Tolle may take umbrage at this (actually he won't because he's too Zen) and it's not about not being in the present moment, however the present moment is charged with both our past and future. The present moment is where the past and future meet. If we redirect our thinking to the past this could have a positive impact on us. Or it may not. My feeling is that the past is over and I cannot change it. Can I learn something from it? Can I learn something about myself? Good. Now move to the present – there I am.

Let me express this in a different way: correlation is not causation. They are two very different lenses – when I did this last week and then that happened, that's a correlation. I am not powerful enough to assume that I can have a predictable outcome!

Let's come back to 'there I am'. The questions that arise are:

What do I want? How do I want to feel? What would bring me joy? As we refine these questions, making them sharper, changing our lens to see more clearly what it is that we want, we can move towards that destination.

What that means is that when we change our focus solutions become more evident and we begin to think in terms of possibilities and options. Then choices start to soar our way. These opportunities and possibilities do not appear while we are looking behind us at the past. That cannot be changed, no matter how many things you think of now that might have helped you back then.

We look back to avoid making the same mistakes, but is the past an indicator of the future? Can the past predict the future? Will the lessons we learn from the past prevent us from making the same mistakes? Does preventative thinking actually stop us attaining our desires because we fear taking risks?

Let's say I have an unexpected credit card payment to make and I don't have the money. It's a big debt for me. I can reflect on everything that has brought me to this and maybe learn something new about myself. This is a good thing, but I want to be debt-free. I want to be capable of repaying this debt. I also want to feel I am good with money. So I now know how I wish to feel. I bring this feeling into the now. I do know how I can pay this debt: option a) I can speak to the bank and arrange a repayment plan, option b) I can get a temporary part-time job, option c) I can rent out my spare room, option d) ….. (fill in the blank). Now you may not like any of these options or others that you have come up with, however you do have a choice. Your choice is do you like feeling incapable of paying off the debt or do you like feeling grateful that you have several different ways to pay it off? This is your 'there and now' feeling.

The here and now is when we are moving towards where we want to be, where I can see myself as an artist, as a parent, as an employee or as a business owner. You are now on a voyage, seeking to empower yourself, and this is the here and now. You are on a high, moving toward your Ithaka. Obstacles are learning opportunities and setbacks are detours.

Step away from the past. It's expired.

Answers Can Dilute Your Truth

Answers are useful when it comes to practical, scientific and objective matters where there can only be one answer. The example that comes to mind is mathematics, where there is only ever one answer to one plus one. Though many of the sciences hold onto single-answer truths such as gravity, there is still a huge gap in the knowledge of absolute truths in medicine and the universe and, of course, the nature of God.

Personal matters require personal responses.

Yet we still seek the one right answer. "Is this the right person for me?", "Does this outfit suit me?", "Have I made the right choice?", "Is there a better option?" Even in the pursuit of the one right answer how are we ever to discern which it is?

The pursuit of the one and only dilutes our personal truth. Our own truth is not absolute, it's personal. It's neither right nor wrong, it's personal. How can we allow ourselves to trust our own ability to find our own solution (not answer), guidance (not answer) and our own signs to follow? I am avoiding the word answer here because answer feels like there is only ever one and that finding it, the perfect, the right, the one and only, is what takes us off our course and dilutes our search for our own truth.

How then do we reinforce our ability to feel assured that our own subjective solution is good enough to act on? Have we enough confidence to follow our own solutions if they go against the grain of socially acceptable norms?

By all means test yourself by raising your doubts. In fact go ahead and Quest them.

At the end of the day there is an inner knowing, a gut feeling that must be pursued. It is compelling and indefinable. You simply know. Even when the results are unexpected and perhaps unwanted, this is your life – you make the mistakes and the specific lessons that come with them are called experience and will help you launch your next decision.

Always pursue your truth, even if you are guided by someone else. Make sure this solution belongs to you. Your life is your own – take control.

Write out your intentions. What do you think you want? Start there. What do you wish to accomplish? Continue this line of questioning. Look for the many ways to move towards accomplishment. How? Feel the accomplishment. Activate your inner guidance system, your intuition. Intuition is deactivated when a goal is the answer and reactivated by imagination when we are seeking our own truth. It is the expression of our most creative and individual self. Pay as much attention to yourself as to anyone else; otherwise you will dilute your own distinctive nature.

⊲ Make Your Mark ⊳

This is a journal-writing exercise to help you relate to your intuition. Write or mind map on the following three words separately: I and me and mine. What do they mean? What does I mean? What does me mean? What does mine mean? When you begin reflecting on these pronouns that have a different way of expressing the idea of self, you may start to wonder who you are. This writing exercise invites the imagination to participate because I am not asking you to write from a linguistic perspective. When you have completed this, compare the results. What are the contrasts? How well do you know yourself and can you begin to sense who you really are?

You Are Still Moving Even When You Are Still

Even when we appear to be doing nothing, we are moving.

Our hearts are beating, our blood is circulating, our minds are reflecting – there is a lot of movement going on. All this movement is subtle, we take it for granted and we are not conscious of our heart beating and our blood circulating, but it's still there happening.

Meditation moves like this. It takes us into zones of quiet - the quiet of a calm mind, the quiet of a still mind - where we can hear the subtleness of our deepest desires that have not yet been given a voice, the ones that would move all the obstacles in their way, like judgement of others, what we think we should be and do and what we do from guilt or fear.

We are always on the move. Even when we sleep we dream. Whether we remember or not, we toss and turn and can be woken up by an unfamiliar sound.

Like dreams, meditation takes us to another state. Pay attention to that state and get to know its nature, what it feels like when you meditate, what happens to your heartbeat and your breath. What are you thinking? Just observe, do not stop to question or judge yourself. Observe yourself when you meditate. Have you any sense of time and if you do how accurate is it? Did 10 minutes feel like a lifetime? Did 20 minutes feel like two?

Become familiar with your different experiences. Which one is real? Are they all real? If they are all real why do you change in each state?

When you find yourself unchanging in any given state then you will have found yourself, your true self, your truer self, for that which does not change is the only higher truth. Our bodies will change. The weather does change. Our opinions change. But the essence remains unchangeable.

Find yourself in your stillness. There's a lot of drama going on there!

◄ Make Your Mark ►

This is a variation on the five minute meditation I introduced in *Hurry Up And Slow Down*. You will need a candle to do this meditation. Either a real candle or you can download a flickering candle image from the Internet. Light the candle and place it 60cm away from you. Sit in a chair, feet on the ground, back elegantly upright, chin slightly tucked so that the crown of your head is aligned to the heavens. Start by paying attention to your breath as you breathe in through your nose and exhale through your nose. As your breath steadies into a rhythm, soften your gaze and begin to follow the tip of the flame. Follow the highest point of the flame as it flickers to the left and right. Keep following this dance with fire for five minutes.

As with the counting meditation exercise, I would like you to keep a meditation journal for 21 days. If you like you can alternate between the counting meditation and this one.

I Deeply Don't Care

There are times when we inadvertently validate other people's opinions by valuing them more than our own. This happens when we allow those opinions to create self-doubt. Why do we care so deeply about anyone else's opinion? And why do we focus on it long after the words have been said, taking offence and feeling bad? At other times, we seek to fight for our position, to correct their opinion simply because it was objectionable to us. Why do we need to set the record straight? Aren't we the record keepers? And if we do know who we are, can another person's opinion of us affect us so badly?

We constantly seek validation, recognition that we are doing good, and we seek affirmation of our positive qualities. We want other people to see and attest to our supreme perfection and justifiable imperfections, for we are taught never to be wrong, especially in public.

Maybe there are two versions of us: the idea of who we are and who we actually are, the unaffected version of ourselves.

You owe it to yourself to discover who you are when you are not affected by external stimuli – opinion or events. Is that possible? *If a tree falls in the forest, and no one is around to hear it, does it still make a sound?*

The idea of who we are is relatively simple. For example, if I consider myself an extraordinary teacher, then I model myself on the archetypal extraordinary teacher and become that. If I see myself as a humble artist sacrificing all for my art, then my behaviour and beliefs will reiterate that. However these are examples of how we want others to view us, examples of character and honour, standing in the community, personal reputation. We spend a lot of time refining these. We go to school to be educated, to speak the part and to think the part. But there is a part of us that remains unspoilt by the accumulation of awards, prizes and accomplishments and that part of us is timeless and never-ceasing.

My soul is the 'I am' of me, the part of me that is timeless. The process of discovering the nature of my soul is the process of congruency, where my heart and mind are aligned, where there is no discord between what my heart feels and my mind thinks. This meeting point is my soul.

My soul shelters my natural state, my individual state of authenticity and unity. My soul is my psychological core. It is my sense of self. Here I cannot be shaken, displaced or pushed aside. I cannot be broken up. There are no answers to my questions, for answers limit the journey. Answers are like full stops, but my soul is a continuum of commas. In this state of being you can experience deeply, not caring about other opinions. 'Deeply not caring' may still hurt a little, that's okay, but deeply not caring will not cause you to need to change. Nor will you need to set the record straight, for you are the record keeper.

'Deeply not caring' is not a place per se. It is not a 'talk to the hand' or 'je m'en fous' or 'whatever' attitude. It says that what you are saying to me or about me will not make me feel small, marginalised or diminished. It cannot weaken me, nor does it strengthen me and though I am being judged, I am witness to my own self. Only I decide if the record needs to be set straight.

This deep place of not caring helps us to create and to be braver in our creation, no matter what others may think.

It is not a matter of ignoring other opinions, good or otherwise, but it is up to us to discern what is our truth, to be mindful and conscious of what opinion may transform us and become an insight for personal growth and what opinion may not matter to us.

Do I want to be defined by the made up thoughts of others? This is right or this is wrong is full stop thinking. Increase the comma's in your thinking for they create a pause, a gap to be explored and somewhere in those gaps is where you will find your truth.

Am I Failing To Understand?

At what point did we come to believe that failure held no value, that it should be a phrase to avoid, never spoken out loud unless followed by 'because', which blames somebody or something else? Thus we are the innocent bystanders witnessing the failure happening to us instead of searching for the undeniable richness of failing. We end up hiding the rewards of failure and driving them into the abyss.

Unhide them!

Life cannot fail you.

Whatever journey you take cannot fail you.

The choices you make cannot fail you.

You are unfailable and therefore cannot be a failure.

Ever.

One of my most challenging art classes is teaching how to draw faces, in particular the self-portrait. It is the Holy Grail of the arts, so for a beginner it contains everything about failure. Failure to identify whose face has been drawn; if you can identify the face then failure to capture the essence, the feel of the sitter. This is not to be outdone by the failure of how you look anyway. There is the inability to see our own beauty and our imaginative way of seeing all our flaws.

Kathy, a newcomer to the arts and a first-time student of mine, said "I'm talking about accomplishments, not gifts." She was responding to what it means to be creative and someone had said she had children. She considered her children gifts; creativity was about accomplishment.

Accordingly, each of us is a gift and the gift bearers are our parents. I do not stop becoming a gift because I have grown up. Let me take this thought a step further.

Is it possible that when I create a self-portrait I am only the instigator? If so, are my accomplishments only gifts? I am having trouble fitting failure into this equation.

What would our lives be like if we allowed failure to reward and not punish us? Would that mean we would seek the rewards? Could we make this a Quest?

We don't fail, we get results that allow us to make new decisions, take new action and create again.

We are not failures, we are creators and we create in whatever circumstances we find ourselves, if we choose to, if we desire it enough.

Maybe that's how we fail: when we don't seek to find the rewards. Therefore we can succeed in failure when we uncover the rewards.

I Think. I'm Feeling.

I think and I feel. It's part of being human. To think and to feel are two different domains that we inhabit and we try to justify one (the feeling domain) by the other (thinking domain). Maybe it's time to give them their own voices, to treat them equally and give them equal weight.

If we do that we will see that we have two perspectives on who we are. One is how we think we are (this is the idea of self, our high dream of self). Then there is the way we actually behave, the way we react to people and events. These automatic responses are generally diametrically opposed to how we think we present ourselves. When this occurs we are incompatible, thinking that we are one person and behaving like another and our idea of who we are will rank higher than our reactive behaviour.

When our behaviour diverges from the idea of who we are, what I call our high dream of ourselves, we do our best to explain and justify that reactive behaviour - that scallywag, wayward and unruly force that pushes through uninvited.

Is this what they call our shadow self, our dark side that comes thrusting forward?

The shadow side of us is what we are not aware of. It catches us unexpectedly, like those times when we over react and we scramble to find ways to agree with it. We want to agree because it is difficult to accept that this strong internal force that erupted, that we could control, could actually be wrong. Could I be wrong?

Our shadow cannot exist without light. Think this through for a moment: light is cast and falls against something – a form, a shape, something solid, an object. What is the object? What are we objecting to? This question is the turnkey to self-awareness. What am I actually objecting to?

I am aware that I am here to create a contrast. I am the creation of contrast, the culmination of light and dark, without which I cannot be in form. If I am that and more my interior journey will bounce between light and dark for they are my navigational markers, showing me the way. Without these markers I have no reason to steer myself in any direction.

I welcome the contrast for neither the high dream nor the scallywag is my true self. They both exist to steer me, if I choose to be steered, towards my true nature.

You're probably wondering now who your true self is, if it is who you think or how you behave or neither. If you were to subtract what you do and how you feel, then who would you be? If you remove your idea of yourself and your opinion of other people, who would you be?

I would *be*. That's what I feel. I think…

Epilogue

This is both the end and the beginning of your journey. You are creative. Your life is a creation. You have insight and inner knowing, wisdom and imagination. Find them and use them together with all the qualities of what it means to be human. Celebrate every day, every moment. Showcase the best in you, find joy in your work and if you can't then find the middle ground. In your relationships seek understanding and find other ways to be understood. Tolerate the consequences of your decisions, the ones you have made and those you have deferred. Do your best always. Try to trust the nature of being human and observe how we participate in a field of energy. We are not here for long; if we recognise this then maybe we can avoid the wasted time of arguing about who is right and seek instead to be kind and to make each other happy. Maybe we can collude for happiness. Maybe we can become paranoid and think that everyone out there is plotting to make us happy. Don't give up on yourself even when others have. You are here. You are here on purpose. You are meant to be here. Don't look outside of yourself to discover the meaning of life. Create your own meaning of your life. You are here on purpose and that means something. Trust that life has meaning even if we don't know what it is. Enjoy this adventure on Earth.

Books That Have Been My Teachers

I am an avid reader and to note all the authors and books that have left a deep impression on me would require the addition of another chapter in this book. I mention these books as they relate to what I have been writing in these pages. These books have stood beside me, whether physically or in the memory of my heart, as I continue to explore this world through words.

Art

Drawing On The Right Side Of The Brain by Betty Edwards
The Artist's Way by Julia Cameron
Secret Knowledge by David Hockney
The Notebooks Of Leonardo da Vinci by Leonardo da Vinci
Abstraction And Empathy by Whihelm Worringer

Positive Psychology & Spirituality

The Power of Intention by Dr Wayne Dyer
The Seven Spiritual Laws of Success by Deepak Chopra
The 7 Habits of Highly Successful People by Stephen Covey

The Four Agreements by Miguel Ruiz
A New Earth by Eckhart Tolle
Tao Te Ching by Lao Tzu
Motivation and Personality by Abraham Maslow
Loving What Is by Byron Katie

Poets & Philosophers & Others

The Essential Rumi by Rumi
Tao: The Watercourse Way by Alan Watts, Al Chung-Liang Huan
The Perennial Philosophy by Aldous Huxley
Meditation As a Contemplative Inquiry by Arthur Zajonc

Acknowledgements

I don't believe I could have learnt so much if I wasn't also a teacher in my life and for this I thank my students and clients who have trusted me and continue to trust me, as a guide to walk alongside their life journey. And for all this teaching I have become a great student, always listening to learn, listening to understand other worldviews and personal stories all of which have become windows into my own life.

I wish to thank Rhianna Walcott, who is like a daughter to me and has been at the beginning, middle and end of this writing journey. She has read the book a gazillion times and after each and every read, would give me a smile and deliver encouraging words. But even more significant than that, Rhianna has, and continues to, believe in me. Gratitude to all who have nudged me along the way to write a book, in particular thank you Kaye Fallick. I still remember the time, many moons ago, when we sat down and wrote out the contents of what my book might look like. To the editors that have spent time on my book and provided me their truthful insights – I thank you. To friends and family who showered me with love and encouragement to ensure that I would bring the best of me to these pages – I thank you. I especially thank Matina Spetsiotis for translating the poem and for encouraging my voice to speak. My gratitude to Luisa Catanzaro who has given freely of her time to check and pedantically cross check every word, comma and apostrophe and ensure that I have produced the best dressed version of this book.

To the many who have taken the five step journey and given me feedback, some of which have been recorded in this book – deep thanks to M. Fox, R. Walcott, L. Catanzaro and G. Steele.

And finally, a very special thank you to Annabel Yau. You have been the one and only and best ever studio assistant and you are irreplaceable.

Praise For You are. That is. Creative

Noula's Quest performances with their 'written-question-only' dialogue challenge and stimulate us to open up vistas and take unexplored pathways (neural?/creative?) for who-or-what-knows unexpected and revelatory outcomes and insights.

~ Barbara Dowse
Curator

This book is a gift to yourself. Noula has distilled so much of her wisdom, guidance and wit, and takes you on a journey of discovery to the heart of your creativity. The exercises and explanations are perfect and digestible leading you to your true nature and purpose on this earth - You Are. That Is. Creative. Read it. NOW.

~ Audra Eng
Corporate Executive

Everyone is creative. But it is a sad fact that most of us lose the joy of our own creativity as we take on adult responsibilities. Noula's book unlocks the spontaneity and colour in your life, your hands and your heart. Embrace it.

~ Kaye Fallick
Author & Publisher
www.yourlifechoices.com.au

Noula has captured the elusive formula for creativity and delivered it intact with uncommon wisdom, wit, candour, compassion and tough love. Her coaching and psychotherapy expertise are woven through relatable personal anecdotes and existential quandaries in a way that democratises the parts of the human condition with which we all grapple while recognising the value of the struggle itself to creativity and helping the reader to harness its power. The practical exercises will remain with you as you go about daily life and serve as resource on which to draw in any situation demanding an 'out of the box' perspective, whether it's coming up with something to paint or hatching a business idea. This is a guidebook for creating, becoming, being and celebrating you.

~ Rebecca Long
Artist & Journalist
www.rebeccalongart.com

About The Author

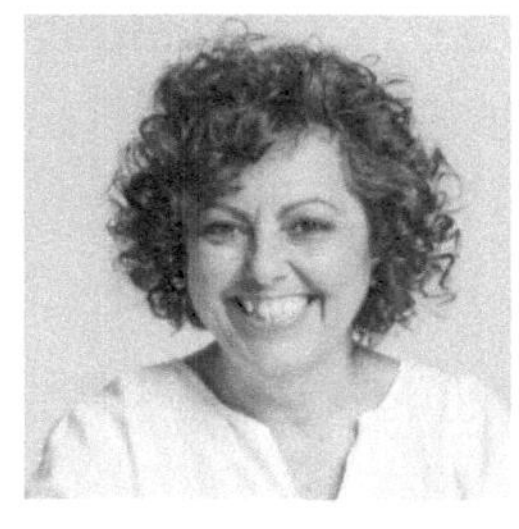

Noula Diamantopoulos is a Sydney based qualified holistic psychotherapist/ coach and a multidisciplinary artist and teacher working across a variety of mediums including performance, sculpture, mosaics, printmaking, painting and encaustics.

For 18 years, in her first career, Noula was an accountant with a Bachelor of Business degree from The University of Technology Sydney, holding the position of international tax manager in the oil and gas industry. It was during the undertaking of her second degree, this time in law, when her sea-change occurred.

In her therapy practice, Noula draws from positive psychology, process orientated psychology, somatic and mindfulness techniques.

In her art and teaching practice, Noula's public art, sculptures and mosaic murals can be seen around NSW. She is the founding and current president of the Mosaic Association of Australia and New Zealand. She runs art workshops in mosaics through her school www.mosaicartschoolofsydney.com and art and mindfulness workshops through www.spontaneouscreativity.com.au

In her corporate practice, Noula creates and facilitates personal development and meditation programs which can be viewed at www.thecorporatebuddha.com.au

She is available for creativity coaching and holistic psychotherapy sessions by Skype. You can send her an email at ilove@nouladiamantopoulos.com

This is Noula's first book.

www.nouladiamantopoulos.com